What the Butler Winked At

Being the Life and Adventures of Eric Horne, Butler

WESTHOLME
Yardley

Originally published in 1923 by T. Werner Laurie
This edition © 2011 Westholme Publishing

Westholme Publishing, LLC
904 Edgewood Road
Yardley, Pennsylvania 19067
Visit our Web site at www.westholmepublishing.com

ISBN: 978-1-59416-530-6
Also available in paperback.

Produced in the United States of America.

Author's Foreword

I have purposely changed the names and localities in the following reminiscences; but doubtless there are people still living who will know they are all true.

Your Humble Servant,

Eric Horne

Contents

CHAPTER I

Now that Old England is cracking up, as far as the Nobility is concerned, who are selling their estates, castles, and large houses, which are being turned into schools, museums, hospitals, homes for weak-minded—things entirely different from what they were built for—it seems a pity that the old usages and traditions of gentleman's service should die with the old places, where so many high jinks and junketings have been carried on in the old days, now gone for ever. The newly rich, who filled their pockets while Tommy was fighting—many of them have bought these fine old estates—are a poor substitute for the real thing. They will send their sons to Oxford or Cambridge, but for generations they will not get the stains off their hands of what they did in the great war; not forgetting who they did.

They may spend their money in giving fêtes, parties, balls, and use every device to get into Society, or what is left of it, but all their doings will only be a sham, a poor substitute. You cannot make a silk purse out of a souced mackerel, neither will they command the same respect; it is simply so much work for so much money, and there the matter ends.

I have lived in the service of a noble family who were ruined by the war; they were such nice people to their servants that, could I have afforded to do it, I would have worked for them for nothing; in fact I did work for them for a year without wages, but they had to continue to reduce the number of indoor servants from twenty-five down to three, outdoor servants in proportion. "How are the mighty fallen!"

Fifty years ago a Lord of the Manor, or a member of the Nobility, was a little tin god on his estate in the country; the people touched their hats to him, or his lady; they looked up to them for advice or help in times of trouble—the villiage people generally living in the same houses all their lives; so that their affairs were known to the people at the Big House. Not so now; people are here to-day and gone to-morrow, are better educated, can think for themselves, and generally only for themselves. No respect is shown when passing each other on the road; the lord in his car would perhaps prefer to run down some of his own villiagers; for class hatred is growing fast; the gulf between rich and poor gets wider and wider, servants seldom remain in one place long enough, even if their employers were so disposed, to take any interest in them.

On crossing Belgrave Square last season, I was comparing the change that had come over things in the course of a few years. One used to see about eight o'clock in the evening gaily comparisoned pairs of horses and carriages, with footmen powdered and breeched, silk stockings, and a lot of pomp and show.

What does one see now?

Gentry need not leave their own houses to go out to dinner, untill within a few minutes that dinner should be on the table. They dart up in a stinking car that sends out noxious fumes; offensive to everyone but themselves.

They dart out of the car, and into the house, as though they had stolen something, and did not want anyone to see them.

Compare this with what it used to be. Two matched footmen would get down, march up to the door, and if a double knocker, both would knock (which they had practised beforehand) then march back to the carriage in a stately fashion, let down the steps, and hand out the ladies. Now, everything is all hurry and scurry. They order out the car, tell the chauffeur to drive to some place; when they get there they want to be somewhere else, when they get *there* they want to be somewhere else; all is unrest; they keep the chauffeur at it sometimes for fifteen hours at a stretch, go to some restaurant and get a snack, then go on again. It does not matter if the chauffeur gets time to get his meals or not: the engine does not get tired, neither must the chauffeur get tired.

English home life is all broken up. The husband may meet his wife at meals, and he may not; most probably not. At any given meal time, or at any entertainment, the chances are that the gentleman will be found dining with a "lady" not his wife, and the lady dining with some gentleman, not her husband: and the chauffeur is waiting outside for hours in the cold and wet.

When one is passing along Piccadilly on the top of a 'bus one can see the "Swells" lounging in their copious chairs, reading the newspapers, and smoking cigars. Pray don't envy them, for half of them go there to get out of range of their wives' tongues, who make it too hot for them to stop at home.

As an instance of what they think of a chauffeur the following occurred this year. They had used the car all day, in the evening the chauffeur asked if he could have the evening off. The "gentleman" asked what he wanted the evening off for.

"To go and see my sick wife. I also have a dead child lying at home," replied the chauffeur.

"You are a damned nusiance, wanting time off. I wanted you to drive me to the theatre, and supper afterwards," replied the gentleman.

Then the chauffeur replied, "You may dam well drive yourself, for I will never drive you another yard."

The inhuman monster. They are nearly all alike. "Self, self, self" again, and if any left, "Self again."

Another amusing incident occurred a few years ago in Bruton Street. I know the lady and I know the chauffeur.

The "lady," when she wanted to tell him something in the car, had the habit of poking him in the back of his neck with the ferrule of her umbrella. One day she called, "Smith" (jab in the back of the neck), "why did you not go the other way?" Soon after (jab), "Now we are here, call at Wilkin's" (jab), "there it is, on the left" (another jab). That was the last, for he drew the car to the side of the street, got out, took off his cap and coat, threw them in the car, and said, "My lady, drive the car yourself. I have had enough of your jabs in the neck." He went away and left her there.

Any chauffeur driving in London has quite enough to do to watch and dodge the traffic, without being jabbed in the back of the neck with an umbrella.

It requires the temper of an angel to take the insults of some of the gentry; not that I suppose an angel would enjoy being jabbed in the back of the neck with an umbrella more than a human being, but there is no accounting for tastes.

When a servant retaliates in this style they should take care to have something to fall back upon. In this case he went and drove for tradesmen. He said, "No more of your gentry for me!" Otherwise they are certain to "down" you; they won't "give you a character," and do all they can to prevent you from earning a living. "What care I how good you be, If you are not good to me." Tradesmen, when they come in contact with them, always tody, bow, and scrape, but they make them pay through the nose for it.

A few weeks ago I happened to be in one of the "Slavey Markets," the place where they hire servants. A man spoke to me: a stranger. He said: "Thank God, I am to have nothing more to do with the gentry. My wife and I have taken a little business. I think some of the gentry ought to be boiled." I replied, "Excuse me from differing from you in a little detail; I think some of them ought to be baked." The gentry would simply laugh at this, for they know they hold the whip hand, every time. They hold all the trump cards, and always win if a servant is the opponent. Do they ever ask themselves this question, "Where did I come from? and why? Where am I going to, and when?"

A certain scientist, a short time ago, valued the material commercial value of the human frame at —Women, four shillings and twopence; men— three shillings and sixpence. The women, having more fat on their frames from which glycerine could be made. Now this is something to"throw ones weight about" on, isn't it? considering God's creatures are all made of the same stuff. But the gentry think they are best china, the poor common clay. But the dressmakers and tailors find the gentry's frames handy to hang their expensive clothes and furs on. Which goes to show that the brain, the soul, the thinking machine, is all that matters; and I know several gentry that has no more brains than a rabbit. They may have them, but they have never had occasion to use them, further than to write out a cheque, take it to the bank, and "carry on." Although in this country one is supposed to be innocent until proved guilty, a servant is generally watched at first untill he or she has proved themselves to be innocent, and honest.

Some butlers delight in besting a mistrustful Bos. I knew one personally. The Bos kept the keys of the wine cellar himself. When he wanted wine out of the cellar he called the butler, handed him the keys, stood at the cellar door, told the butler to get wine out of a certain bin. The butler brought out the bottle carefully in front of him,

but he had another bottle in his coat-tail pocket
for himself; he locked the cellar door, handed the
Bos the keys, and all was well.

Certainly there is a vim about "doing down"
a mistrustful devil like that, and as to the wine,
it was like stolen kisses, "Sweet."

A rather curious, well thought out plan of rob-
bery happened in Berkeley Square some years
ago, at a titled lady's house. The footman had
been given notice to leave as he was unsuitable.
After he had left a man called at the front door
with a parcel of silk, to be taken to the lady's-
maid at the top of the house: he was to wait for
an answer. The new footman asked the man to sit
down in the hall and wait. The footman came
down with the parcel of silk saying, "It must be
a mistake, the lady's-maid knew nothing about
it." The man said he would take it back to the
shop.

When her ladyship went to dress for dinner she
found her jewel case ripped open, and all her
jewellery gone. This is how it was worked.
While the new footman was gone upstairs with
the silk the man in the hall opened the door and
let in the old footman who, knowing the ways of
the house, hid himself in the dining-room, either
behind a curtain or under the table, until he heard
the new footman let the man (his confederate)
out, and heard the new footman go downstairs.

(He knew the ways of the house, and had watched her ladyship go out in her carriage.) He then crept upstairs, did the trick, came down, and let himself out. But, not being professionals at the game, they did not know how to dispose of the swag, and were caught trying to dispose of some of the jewellery at a pawn-shop. The old footman afterwards explained how it was done. Their enginuity was worthy of a better cause.

While I am on the subject of robberies I will here set down a story about burglary. I was in a hunting box in Bucks. for the season. Burglaries had been frequent at several houses all round the county: one happened very near us. One night the kitchenmaid came running to me and said, "There is someone in my bedroom, the door is fastened and I can't get in." I went outside and saw that her window was open. I sent down to the hunting stables, asking that all the grooms and stable helpers should come to the house, arming themselves with hay-forks, sticks, and shovels. I got my revolver, placed the men outside the window, while I and a footman went up to the door inside the house. I tried the door, but it would not open. I shouted, "You are surrounded, and bound to be taken; you had better come out and give yourself up. I have a revolver, and shall have first shot." No answer! So the footman and I put our shoulders to the door to burst it open. I told him to spring back to the side of the door, in case the burglar should shoot. We pushed our hardest, the door gave way, we sprang back and listened. Not a sound. We then went into the room, looked under the bed, in the wardrobe, up the chimney, but found nothing. On examining the door we found that a corner of the carpet had come unfastened, and so held the door fast. The result of all this was I had to stand a gallon of beer, to compensate the grooms and helpers for being disturbed in their rest.

I now propose to give the history of my life, from the very beginning, giving all the incidents that has happened in the course of fifty years' service amongst the Nobility and Aristocracy of this country.

How many thousands of people pass the doors of the gentry in the streets and squares in the West End of London, or see their country mansions, have any idea of the internal workings of these houses?

I propose to open the doors of some of them, and what I will show you about gentleman's service, I hope will at least be interesting.

I was born of very poor, but very prowd parents not very far from Southampton. When I say prowd I don't mean the three P.'s: pride, poverty, and pianos: but the pride of working, and paying one's way, and not borrowing a half-penny from anyone: though I own it must have been a tight squeeze at times for my mother and father to find enough for us to eat, and clothes to our backs, also pay for our education. I had one brother and two sisters, another was born before myself but died in infancy.

My mother was certainly from a better family than my father, in education; and in every sence of propriety, a lady in disposition without wealth. In the early part of the eighteenth century very few people, perhaps ten in every hundred of the working class could read and write. There were no board schools then: education had to be paid for by the pupils, or their representatives.

My mother helped me in everything I ever learnt. As soon as I could toddle, I went to an old Dames school. The old lady had come down in the world, so took infants to learn them the alphabet, at three-pence per week, and perhaps there was another consideration in it: she had care of the infants, and so allowed the mothers to get on with their work, which was certainly worth three-pence per week.

My mother's father had a farm near Southampton. She and her brothers and sisters used to ride to a good school in Southampton on ponies. Eventually the farm was burnt down. It was not insured. Insurance was not so common in those days. So the family was scattered. She and her sisters going into service. My mother went as lady's-maid to two ladies in the town in which I was born, remaining with them till she got married. My father worked for the same employers for more than twenty-five years.

One has very little recollection of what happened the first two years of one's life, but I must have been about that age. I recollect being allowed to play in our little parlour (a room kept sacred for Sundays only) the occasion being that I had taken the medicine (we used to call it "physic").

My mother always gave us periodically a dose of rhubarb and jalap a very nasty concoction. She put it in our mouths and held our noses, so that we were forced to swallow it when we took the next breath. That is the first thing on this earth that I can remember. I was allowed to play in the parlour with an old wooden horse, on wheels, minus head or tail: it had a red stripe round its body, but it had a fascination for me. My mother used to help to keep the wolf from the door by keeping the schools swept and clean, for a few shillings a week, probably not more than three. She also went to the Vicar's house to work, perhaps one day a week, for about eighteen pence and her food. I feel sure she often went short of food and nourishment herself in order that her children should have enough to eat.

I remember asking her what was the meaning of the word "shubby." She said she had never heard it. But I said, "They sing it in church. As it was in the 'ginning, is now, and ever shubby." An explanation followed.

At that time the effect of the Russian War was still felt, especially by the poor, bread being a shilling a loaf. My mother had a strain of the fighting blood in her veins, for nearly all her relations were sailors who fought in the old "wooden walls" of England, one being a Quartermaster, and fought under Nelson. I remember a Bible we had, on the fly leaf the Quartermaster had made notes of the sea battles, and the names of ships that went into action, and names of enemy ships taken.

In after years I have heard my mother say how prowd she was when he took her to London after the Russian War, in his Quartermaster's uniform. She told me the Russians, who had been prisoners, drank the oil out of the street lamps.

When I was old enough to go to the boys' school I began at the bottom class. Somehow I took to learning like a new-fledged duckling taking to water, and greatly assisted by my mother, who could answer every question I wished to ask, I could with safety be backed to be in the "first three" in my class.

In after years, when about twenty years of age,

I went to a phrenologist, "just for fun." I did
not speak to him a single word, to give him any
idea as to what or who I was, but at once sat in
the chair. He "felt my bumps," and said I was
either fit to be an actor, a lawyer, or a parson, but
fate destined that I should be neither. I continued at school untill I was strong enough to be
useful to somebody, and do some sort of work,
probably at the age of ten or twelve, working half
a day, and going to school half a day. I was also
pleased to earn a shilling or two to give to my
mother.

Our schoolmaster was one of the best. He
found out I had a good voice, and got me in the
Church Choir, where there were sixteen boys and
twelve men, and a good organist who tried to drive
some of the mysteries of music and harmony into
us: he might almost have had sixteen monkeys to
deal with.

We went to practice two evenings a week. The
church at that time was lit by colza oil lamps and
candles. We used to play some awful games on
the organist. When the practice was finished us
boys would rush down the stairs, through the
belfry, after putting a tin tack through the rim
of his top hat, fastening it to the seat, then putting
out all the lamps, leaving him to come down in
the dark, also putting one of the bell ropes across
the stairs.

I do not propose to appear as a model boy—far from it—for if not the ringleader of any mischief that was going on I was always willing to take part in it, and took my punishment, in the shape of a cane and numbers of lines to write, with a certain amount of pluck. Being near Portsmouth, gunpowder had a rare fascination for us, but how to get it? That was the question. Most of us used to be allowed a halfpenny a week pocket money. We would agree to go seperately to the ironmonger's shop and ask for a penny-worth of it, "to blow out mother's copper" on washing days, or a wasp's nest. We were generally successful, though the shopmen must have known we had some mischief on hand.

Most of us had small brass cannons. I had one six inches long, but we used to put too much gunpowder into them. One day I fired it off outside the back door of our house, touched it off with a red-hot poker, but I never saw the cannon again. It either burst, or went up in the air.

On our visits to our uncle's farm I always covetted an old horse pistol that hung on the wall of the kitchen. Eventually he gave it to me, cautioning me to be careful; he also gave me the mould for leaden bullets. The pistol is sixteen inches long. Any sort of metal that would melt was brought into requisition, sometimes the table-spoons were missing to make bullets.

One day I heard a terrific bang. I saw my brother had fired it off at a chalk bird he had drawn on the lavatory door at the bottom of the garden. I ran down to see how near he was to his mark, and asked him if anyone was inside the lavatory. He said, "I don't know." With much trepidation we opened the door, there was no one there; but the bullet had made a round hole through the door and knocked a brick out of the wall at the back. Had there been anyone there they would have had a hole through, about the waist line.

Those old guns and pistols were fired by a percussion cap. There was no absolute certainty of their going off when the trigger was pulled, but would often mis-fire, or hang fire.

On one occasion my brother and I were shooting thrushes in the orchard. The gun mis-fired. I took it from my shoulder to put on another cap when the gun went off, the shots passing my brother by a few inches. I thought I had shot him.

The reader may say, "What has all this got to do with gentleman's service?" I simply want to show what sort of metal the writer is made of. If the readers will only have a little patience I will take them through gentleman's service right enough, in every grade from hall-boy to butler and house steward, and from scullery maid to housekeeper. They will then see why so very few select the job in order to get a living.

I must have been about eight or nine years old when a party of boys went fishing for minnows in a river. The tide did not come up from the sea as far as our fishing ground, but only as far as a flour mill—the river water was collected in an immense mill pond—and drove the mill when the tide was down, twice in every twenty-four hours. On the landward end of the mill pond a bridge spanned the river, of twenty feet high, on five arches. Here we fished, with our sticks and string and a pennyworth of small fish-hooks and worms, turning our knickers up as far as possible and wading in.

I happened to be on the top of the bridge, in the centre. I shouted something down to my chums. At that moment my rod slipped out of my hand and fell into the river. I shouted, "save my rod," and lost my ballance, and over I went. The next thing I saw was several people standing round me. I was laid on my back on a red brick floor in somebody's house. When I opened my eyes somebody said, "He will be all right now!" From that day to this I never knew who saved me: my only trouble was that I had skinned my knuckles against the buttress of the bridge as I fell. I was told to run away home. Outside, I found my chums waiting expectantly; so we all went towards home. But what about my wet clothes? They would tell the tale. So, on crossing a rough piece of ground called the Oggplat (why it was called by that name I never knew) and as the sun was very hot, I took off all my clothes and laid them on the grass to dry, one of my chums lent me his jacket as a footpath crossed the Oggplatt. When we thought my clothes were dry I put them on, and we went home. My mother asked what made me so late for tea. I laid low, and said nothing.

I was sitting on a stool having my tea, which had been put aside for me, when some woman knocked at the door and asked how her son was. Mother said: "Which one." She replied: "Eric" (that's me) "didn't you know he was drowned in the river?" "No," said my mother, "he is in the kitchen having his tea." That gave the game away. Mother soon had my partly dried clothes off, and she sent me to bed.

I must have had phneumonia, or some other fine thing, for I was jolly bad the next day or so. I remember asking my mother, as she sat down by my little bed, if I was going to die. She replied, "No: I hope not." Anyhow, no doubt it saved me from a good thrashing, as I was told not to go fishing; and my father could lay it on a bit thick for disobedience. I did not get much of it, but what I did get I deserved, and more.

All this time I was making good progress at school. I passed the examinations as they periodically came up. Our schoolmaster was a good one. He would not allow any bullying. If he saw a big boy bullying or striking a smaller boy he would call me or one of the others, and say, "Go and give so-and-so a good licking," and then discreetly disappear. I would go up to the bully in the playground and ask him why he struck a smaller boy than himself. This led to a "few words," then suddenly the cry, "A fight," a ring was quickly formed, a line drawn on the gravel with a boot (why, I don't know, except that we had to toe it) then we set to work. If one of us got knocked down it was unlawful for the other to strike him when down, but if both were on the ground, it was lawful to go on fighting. When the schoolmaster thought I had given him enough he would appear. Both of us had to go up for punishment for fighting. I got light strokes on the hand with the cane, the other fellow got heavy strokes, and a good lecture about bullying small boys.

My father, in his trade, had to hire and pay a boy to assist him. So I suppose he thought as I was clever enough to get into plenty of mischief I was clever enough to assist him. I was taken from school half a day. Every morning my father would leave the house at half-past five. I left it at half-past six, in order to begin work at

seven o'clock.   My father was not so well educated
as my mother.   He could manage to read and
write and keep his accounts.   He had strong opinions on politics, and things in general; and was
always ready to back up his opinions with his fists,
if necessary.   One idea he was very hot on.   He
would say that Church and State walked hand-
in-hand.   The State would punish you bodily for
any offences against the law.   The Church would
threaten you with eternal damnation after you are
dead; and that is the way they keep the people in
order.   Well, if you lift the curtain, he was not
very far wrong.

Nowadays, if anyone throws their empty lobster
tins over into the neighbors' gardens, and pokes
their tongues out at each other, they take a summons out and you appear at the Police Court.

In 1840 they had a better and quicker way of set-
tling the matter.   My father would say, "Just step
outside for a few minutes.   We will soon settle it."
He could use his fists a bit.   He also thought he
could dance a hornpipe.   He could, in an old-
fashioned way.   When he was a young man the
Lord of the Manor would put up prizes at holiday
times for competitions in boxing, single-stick (the
winner had to make his opponent's blood run an
inch to win), also sides at a cricket match on the
village green, and all kinds of old-fashioned
games; to end up with a supper at the Inn, after

which the "ladies" would join in a mazy dance.
Country dances and a polka was the extent of the
programme. He thought he was a champion, and
an authority as to how it ought to be done.

He was a keen sportsman, a remarkably good
shot. He had two guns, one had a barrel five feet
long, the other shorter. About that time all the
commons, also the foreshores at low tide, were
taken over by the Government. People could no
longer turn their cows, horses, and pigs freely to
graze, and roam free of cost. Give my father a
gun, and something to shoot, and he was happy. I
have known him take a shot at a starling, or even
a sparrow in flight, during his dinner hour. I
never knew him to miss. The restrictions made it
difficult to get a bit of sport. I have known him
to take his gun to pieces, put it inside his coat, and
off down to the foreshore on a winter's night, for
wild ducks and geese. He seldom came back
empty-handed, he would bring them down with his
long muzzle-loading gun. His idea was that God
sent these things for all to enjoy, all wild beasts
and birds.

I have known him when he had his gun inside
his coat going down the road, on seeing a policeman coming up, to turn back and go another way.
He would never allow me to go with him on these
excursions.

He used to tell me that when he was a young

man he had a dog called "Bob." Father would place nets in the rabbit runs along the road, then he would say, "Go on, Bob." The dog would take a half-circle of about two hundred yards on the opposite side of the hedge. It was not long before he had his Sunday dinner in his pocket. If anyone should come along father was out enjoying the evening air, what ho! If he had a gun licence I never saw it.

He used to go to church on Sunday evenings. His dress was: half Wellington boots, that went up under his trowsers; a black satin waistcoat, with coloured flowers, hand-worked roses, I think, down the front; his shirt collar was turned up, and a long silk neckkerchief, put first round the front, crossed at the back, brought to the front, and tied in a bow; a black coat; and top hat, not extra smooth; he also carried a stick.

He was very fond of my reading the weekly newspaper to him in the evening when he came home from work. Then he would criticise the politicians and their doings. His mother's house was burnt when he was a young man. He told me that if a house or habitation was built on common land, between sunset and sunrise with smoke coming out of the chimney, that place was yours. He and his brothers did it for their mother. I have seen it. Principally made of clay and wattle, and what bricks they could collect from the ruins of the burnt house. I think he called it "Key-hold." There was just two rooms and a brick floor.

My youngest sister was quite a little housewife in her way. She had a fascination for nursing babies after she got too old for dolls. One day she had borrowed a neighbour's baby to look after. She sat it on the floor while she did the housework, my mother having gone out to work. I was play-ing hockey with some boys in the road, when I saw her come to the front door and shout to me, "I am all a-fire." By the expression of her face I thought she was laughing, but it was the contortion of fear: then I saw the smoke. I bounded over the garden wall, took her indoors, and with the short brush she had been sweeping with I beat out the flames. She had been sweeping up the hearth, and in turning round with the fender the back of her frock caught alight. I soon had all her smouldering clothes off, and called in a neighbour. Her back was burnt, and all her hair was burnt off. I was only just in time. But, curious to relate, after the advice of a doctor, she had a beautiful lot of hair, which grew on a scalp that before looked like a bladder of lard.

Just one or two more of my school-day esca-pades then I am off into gentleman's service.

We attended choir practice every Wednesday and Friday. It happened that the estate steward and estate carpenter of a large gentleman's house, just outside the town, got themselves in bad repute through women, or no woman, something of that sort; us boys did not know exactly what it was, but the people broke all the windows in the steward's house in High Street. The affair caused a great commotion in the town.

Now, choir boys could not be out of an affair like this, so we agreed to give the carpenter, whose house we passed on our way home from practice, a volley of stones at his front door, then all bolt home as fast as our legs could carry us.

That passed off all right, but the next practice night we agreed to repeat the dose. We were bad stratigists, for the carpenter must have known it was the choir boys; all other boys had gone to bed at that time—9.30 P. M.—in a country town, also he could see the lights in the church at the end of the street. We were all ranged up, each with a stone in his hand, waiting for the word "Fire," when out from the side of the house popped the carpenter in his slippers. We scattered. I accidently fell off the kerb and rolled into the gutter. I heard the carpenter run past me, chasing the others. I got up and went another way home, thinking I was lucky. My father and mother and all went to bed early, as they had to get up early. My supper was always left covered up with the table cloth, also the back door was left unlocked for me. I locked the door and crept up to bed.

My mother called out from the next room, "Is that you, Eric?" I replied, "Yes." She asked, "Have you had your supper?" I said, "I was not hungry." I thought I had got out of that job all right, when, "Bang, bang," someone was at our front door. My father said, "Who is that?" and told me to answer the door. I said I was in bed and did not want to go down. He asked, "What mischief have you been up to now?" He got out of bed and opened the window, and said, "Yes, what do you want?" The carpenter said, "Your boy has been throwing stones at my door. I shall take a summons out against him in the morning!" I said, "I was about to throw, but you came out too quick, so I didn't throw the stone." "Oh, but George Coles (another choir boy) said it was you."

After a great deal of jaw my father shut the window and said to me, "I have done with it; now you must take the consequences." I laid in bed and thought to myself, "Well, you have put your foot into it at last, my lad." But I felt sorry for George Coles—the first chance—though he was a bigger boy than me. When I woke up the next morning it dawned on me what had happened. I expected every minute to hear the policeman knock at the door with the summons.

At dinner time nothing had happened. My mother tried to perswade me to go to the carpenter's house, and catch him at home in his dinner hour, and beg his pardon. But I said, "I did not throw a stone, he came out too quick for us. Why should I beg his pardon for what I did not do?" Mother said, "He firmly believes you did, be advised by me and go: it will be best." Reluctantly I went round to his back door and stood in a little stone yard, thinking how I should begin. I could hear the knives and forks clattering inside. He must have heard and seen me. Presently he came out and said, "What do *you* want?" I said, "I have come to beg your pardon for throwing stones at your door last night; but I didn't throw, you came out too quick, but I won't do it again." I suppose the absurdity of my speech tickled his imagination, for he said, "All right, don't."

He had two boys—they both attended the same school as myself—they came out, and their father went off to work. The boys said, "Have you seen our young chickens? Come up the garden and look at them." They were only a day or two old, there were about a dozen of them. I said I should like to have one of them, a little yellow and black one; so I gave the oldest boy a penny, which I had got from my mother by way of a bribe to beg the father's pardon. Having bought the chicken we all went towards the school together. The "all-in" bell rang. I rushed indoors, put the chicken in a basket with a lid, down by the side of the fire, and off to school. When I came out I fed the chicken.   My mother could not make out what it was "Chirp, chirp," all the afternoon.   She thought it was a cricket on the hearth.   Then came explanations.   Before I had finished explaining, "Bang, bang," came on the front door.   It was the carpenter.   He said, "Your boy is a dam nusiance, first he throws stones at my door, now he gives one of my boys a penny for one of my chicken; the eggs cost more than that."   I had to give the chicken up, and lost my penny, but had the consolation of knowing the boy got a thrashing for selling me the chicken.

Just one more, then I have finished with school tales.

About half a mile from the school there were some clay pits, where the clay had been dug out for making bricks.   It having been a wet season these pits were full of water.   On the side was a wide plank, about eighteen inches across, and of great length.   One day, after dinner, eight or ten of the oldest boys thought it would be a fine game to launch this plank, all standing on it, pushing it along with poles.   The end of the plank was on land.   When all was ready someone gave the order to push off: we did.   Some boys wobbled one way, some the other, the end of it was the plank capsized, we were all struggling in the water.   After all had swam ashore, clambering up the bank, we found ourselves in a fine pickle, wet through and our clothes covered with yellow clay.

At this time about a dozen of the oldest boys, who were nearly ready to leave school for good, had to attend an advanced class, held in the committee room, by the headmaster, on subjects as dry as dust, mathematics, ancient history, Latin, grammer, etc. On this occasion one of the boys said, "There goes the first bell." Away we scuttled as fast as we could run. Got there just in time. Most of us went to the committee room and sat down at our desks. The headmaster came in. He told us to form a half circle round his desk; then the trouble began. He asked, "What is that on your clothes?" On closer inspection he saw we were wet through. He went out of the room; in a few minutes he returned with a cane in his hand; called each by name, as he stood by the door, gave us three or four of his hardest strokes, told us to go home to change our clothes, and come back. We got a few hundred lines to write out over that escapade.

The examination time was drawing near, but I did not fear it. The inspectors came down. I passed out the best boy of the school, on all subjects, and got the first prize for that year.

CHAPTER II

THERE were no such thing as scholarships for boys in those days. Even if there had been I could not have accepted one, as I was now a big boy of twelve years, eating my parents out of house and home. They wanted me to earn my own living, or something towards it. I still continued to sing in the church choir. I had a strong, sweet voice, and at this time was leading treble. The organist's son had a sweet voice, but not so strong as mine, he had to sing second treble. I used to glory in singing my best, also to hear the tenors, counter tenors, and altos on my left, over my head, and the bass roaring away on my right. The alto would lean over and say, "Go it, Eric!"

Once a year we gave a concert at the Town Hall, and very prowd I was to see my name, "Leading Soprano," on the bills, all over the town. On one occasion, after the organist's son and I had sung a duet, it is usual for the pianist to play a little twiddly bit after we had finished the duet, then for us to bow both together, but as soon as the singing part was finished I "went off," but seeing my mistake went back and made another bob, and, oh! the white gloves.

My mother had made me an Eton jacket, (I fear it was a moth-eaten jacket) out of one of my father's old coats.

At Christmas we went carol singing, carrying a note from the Vicar. The people would then ask us in, when we would sing. They would give us cake and fruit, perhaps a drop of ginger wine, and a few shillings. The men went by themselves, and sang glees, madrigals, and catches.

On these occasions the older boys would endeavour to give the younger ones the slip, and lose them. I was served so when I first joined the choir. I went home, but my father took me back, found out at which house they were singing at, opened the front door and pushed me in.

My father did not require a boy to help him in the winter, and as his trade only led one into a "cul de sac," my mother was more ambitious for me. My eldest sister had already gone out to service.

So the schoolmaster got me a job with a friend of his, a printer and stationer. I had to get there by seven o'clock, sweep out, and dust, open the shop, take down the shutters. After breakfast I went up with the printers, inked the type with a roller—they used to print by hand press then; after he had taken an impression, and rolled it back I inked the type for the next. There were four or five boys. We all had to meet the eleven o'clock train from London, and carry bundles of newspapers into the hotel stable. The head boy would allot so many of each sort to all of us: we folded each paper on the floor, then off on your round, as per list, but I soon got to know who had the different papers without the list. The quicker we got round the sooner we had finished for the day. I got three shillings a week, and was prowd to hand it over to my mother. My round covered five miles. I still attended school in the evenings. My brother got a job at a grocer's shop: he was a clever kid, but not so "lively" as myself.

Of course, as is usual, about this age, I had a sweetheart, a pupil of the girls' school adjoining. I fancy I must have used more than my share of our weekly allowance of hair oil. For, when you see a boy begin to be particular about washing his neck, polishing his boots at the heels, and using the clothes brush a bit, you may be sure there is a girl on the horizon.

Some of the boys, as they left school, went to Portsmouth, and got a job as officer's servants, or something of that sort. Anyhow, when they got leave, and came home, dressed in a blue suit, short jacket, black buttons with crown and anchor on them, cheesecutter cap with badge, white shirt front, and little black tie in a bow, it nearly drove me crazy. I asked my mother if I could not be one of them. She said, "No." All her brothers had been drowned at sea, so she would not let me go.

When I was at the printers I often used to see a page boy, with his three rows of buttons down the front of his jacket, riding a donkey, with a post-bag slung across his shoulders. He worked at an old Admiral's place a mile out of town, and rode the donkey to the Post Office twice a day. I envied him. I thought I should like to ride that donkey.

But when I saw him, about Christmas time, I think it was, he was going along the street, loaded with postbag and parcels wherever they could be hung on to him. I suppose the donkey objected to the extra load, for the donkey bucked and pitched him over its head. There he lay, struggling in the mud, and took a bit of sorting out among the parcels and other things. So I thought that does not look very dignified. I don't think I should care for his job after all.

At that time boys, to learn a trade, had to be apprenticed for five or seven years, perhaps be given a little pocket money, but no wages.

My father could not afford to do that.

After working for the printer for some time I got a regular place with a doctor, a friend of the Vicar. I had to look after a black pony, help the groom-gardener, who had a cob and riding horse, and in the garden. I used to help him when I was not out with the doctor in his pony carriage. He had a daughter, aged about fourteen. I used to think she was such a lovely creature; she often came with us in the pony carriage when home on holidays from school. Her father was a widower.

To give an idea what a little fellow I was. When I left the pony's head the doctor used to drive on, but I could not get my foot high enough to reach the step to get into the "dickey" behind; but I used to cling hold and swing myself up somehow. The doctor never looked back to see if he had left me behind or not. Often the young lady would hand me back an orange or an apple. I think the doctor must have had a good private income, as he kept maidservants, and a footman in livery. It was a nice place, with lawn and large kitchen garden. I also used to take round the medicine, and get my meals and sleep at home.

My younger brother had by this time left school and got a job in a grocer's shop. We both slept in the same bed. I used to say to him: "Your clothes does smell strong of coffee." He replied, "Well, that's better than smelling of physic."

The footman where I worked was the most dare-devil that ever I knew: a thorough good servant, tall, fair, and slim. I was not supposed to do any indoor work, but he would make me clean the knives; he would lock me in the boot hole till I had cleaned them.   One day I would not do something he wanted; he caught me, and held the part I sit on in front of the open kitchen fire, and then took me out in the yard and sat me down in the snow.   He would do all sorts of things to tease the gardener.   One day it led to a fight in the stable yard.   I stood up in the wheelbarrow to see fair play.

In the summer, at seven o'clock each morning, I had to bring in the two ponies from the meadow. I was told to catch them and bring them in one at a time.   The groom-gardener would not begin work till eight o'clock; arrive just in time to sit down to the kitchen breakfast, though he was not supposed to, it was a regular thing.   I had to groom the black pony: she and I got great friends. She would follow me about like a dog, take a piece of sugar out of my mouth, and drink beer out of a glass.   One morning, I suppose I was late, I caught both ponies to bring them in both together. On shutting the gate I suppose it touched them. I dropped the seive of oats, one pony went one way, the other in the opposite direction, at full gallop, with their halters dangling.   Here was a pretty pickle.   Which pony should I go after? The groom met one of them, on his way to work, in one part of the town.   The other went off down the High Street, and was brought back by the blacksmith, and I got a whiging.

But I was perfectly happy in my boyish way while there. Everybody was so nice and homely, especially when I had to pull up the weeds among the fruit trees and strawberry beds when they were ripe. But above all was the cricket matches, played in a large field, seperated from the garden wall only by a footpath. I remember the year when eleven played twenty-two, the eleven against all England. W. G. Grace was in his prime then. I think the eleven won. The field was enclosed by eight-feet boards all round it, so that no one could see the play without paying. But we had a grand stand of our own. With the aid of a short ladder we climbed on to the roof of the chicken house, and had a fine view. Crowds came from every town for miles round to see the match. The cricket ground has now been built on.

The Vicar and the Doctor were great friends. Every night the Vicar came to smoke and drink whiskey toddy. In the morning I had to take "The Times" to the Vicar's house, after the doctor had finished with it, on my way home to breakfast. The Vicar was a queer tempered old fellow. On Monday mornings he attended school for our Scripture lesson. We used to say of him:

> "Old Parson Jones is a very good man,
>   He goes to Church on Sundays,
>   To pray to God to give him strength
>   To whack us all on Mondays."

And I have seen him thrash boys with his ash
stick most unmercifully, almost brutal. His clerk
was gardener as well, a tall man who walked with
his eyes always on the ground. In the Vicar's
carriage drive was an almond tree. I was curious
as to whether there were any almonds in the pods,
so one morning I climbed the tree and was laid out
on a branch over the carriage drive when I heard
footsteps approaching. I laid dogo: he passed
underneath me. I could have touched his hat, but
he did not see me.

When it was the cook's day out at the Vicarage
my mother used to go there to assist. One morning, thinking to give the other servants a treat, she
made some apple dumplings, and put them in the
flour tub, covering them up. Then she went upstairs to assist making the beds, etc., as there was
a large family. On arriving back to the kitchen
she saw all the apple dumplings in a long row on
the kitchen table. Mrs. Vicar had been on the
rummage while my mother had been upstairs. So,
instead of the apple dumplings being eaten in the
kitchen, they found their way to the dining room
and were eaten there.

I often used to do errands for the cook when
going to the town. One day she popped a rhasp-
berry tart in my basket as I went out. It was an
open tart; I popped it in my mouth. It was boiling hot, just out of the oven. It took the skin off

the roof of my mouth. I can never see or smell rhaspberries without thinking of that tart, and that was fifty years ago.

I was always very fond of lemons. I could not see one unless I had a desire to suck it dry. There was generally half a lemon in the pantry that came off the grog tray: I had a go at it. The footman noticed this. One day he filled the half lemon with cayenne pepper and went out, but returned the next minute. My mouth was on fire, I wanted to bolt, but he held me, saying, "I knew you would do it." The footman would make up a mixture of vinegar, salt, mustard, Worcester sauce, lemon juice, and all sorts of stuff, and try to make the errand boys who came to the house to drink it. One morning he came with me to catch the ponies in the meadow, we twisted the halter in their mouths, mounted, and galloped round the meadow; of course I fell off.

After being there for some time the footman left. He got married, and went to London, in service there. The Doctor said he would take me indoors in his place. The cook got hold of me; she gave me a good scrubbing down with soap and hot water. I was only a young boy, or I might have blushed. This was my first step into captivity.

Here was a young, healthy boy, with a good education, with any amount of health, spirits and

energy, with a determination to do as the schoolmaster had taught us. To play the game: be
truthful, honest, and never to do a mean action: in
fact to be a nature's gentleman. I thought to
myself, "Well, I mean to get to the top; there
seems to be nothing else for me but gentleman's
service."

Why not get to be the King's butler? Then I
thought of Pharoh's butler, but on referring to the
chapter I found it was all right: it was Pharoh's
baker whose carcase was thrown out for the birds
to pick. Not the butler. No doubt, had I been
apprenticed to a trade I should have made my
mark in the world, some trade that required clever-
ness and brains. Any fool could learn to be a
servant, providing he had no spirit or will of his
own, and did what he was told, and be meek, humble, submissive. I have often wished I had a
trade, making something, or doing something, and
only being paid by results: the more work I did the
more pay I got. If no work, no pay. Here
would be something worth living for. For although I have lived in the service of some of the
best families in the land (and how near I got to
being the King's butler my tale will unfold) I consider my life to have been simply thrown away,
wasted.

Now I had to begin to learn the mysteries of
indoor service, which was as a sealed book to me,

but, being very quick, I soon began to see what was wanted in the dining room.   The footman had put me through a good deal of the pantry work, as he was not too fond of work himself.   I had to leave the choir, as I could not get away for practice, or on Sundays for that matter.   Still, I was happy enough, the other servants treated me well, I got better food and lodgings than I got at home, and I was growing fast into a chubby, blue-eyed, curley-haired lad, and began to take pride in my appearance.   But I was like a young, rollicking puppy, "I had all my troubles to come."

When I was in the gardens I took a small sucker from a high holly hedge and planted it in our little flower bed in front of our house at home.   The next time I went home the holly twig was not there.   I enquired, and found that a boy who lived a few doors away, had taken it, and planted it in his own front garden.   I pulled it up and took it back to where it was before, then waited till the boy came out.   I tackled him, we had a fight, I soon settled him.

The holly twig was not disturbed again, but in years grew nearly as high as the house.   My mother had to have it cut down, as it kept so much light from the windows.

I remained with the Doctor till he gave up the house, and left the town.   He sent to ask my mother to come and see him.   He wanted to know

if he could do anything for my future. I said I
wanted to go to sea, if not in the Royal Navy, the
Merchantile Marine, for I had read a lot of sea
tales, "The King's Own," "Robinson Crusoe," and
a lot more of Captain Marriat's books. But my
mother would not consent. In the end nothing
was done for me. The Doctor left the town, after
everything was sold, and I went home.

Some years after, when I was at Eastbourne, I
saw a young lady in a bath chair. Surely I know
that beautiful face, I thought. It was the Doctor's daughter. She died shortly afterwards, of
what they called the decline. No one mourned her
more than I did, for she appeared to me to be an
angel on earth.

I was not long unemployed, for an old General,
or Captain, I think he was of His Majesties' Body
Guard, sent for me. I went to see him—it was
near my former place, and I suppose they had seen
me about while I was with the Doctor. They engaged me as their footboy, put me into footman's
livery (I never wore page's buttons). But, oh!
what a place! The old Captain had married a
second wife, young enough to be his daughter: she
was all mustard. After I had put away the breakfast things I had to go into the kitchen garden and
dig up large tracts of rough ground with a spade
till it was time to lay the lunch, when I had to put
on the livery and prepare for afternoon visitors.

Which reminds me of an old Scotch lady who got hold of a raw Scotch boy and tried to train him as a page boy. She dressed him in kilts on special occasions when she had company. On one such occasion he popped his head round the drawing room door and asked: "D'ye require me to wear the kilts, or my ain breeks, the day?"

The food was very poor and scarce. But, talk about "Swank," on Sundays I had to carry her church books behind her, dressed in livery, follow her down the aisle, place the books in her pew, then go to my own place. When the service was ended I had to go and get the books, and follow her back to the house, which was of walking distance, and, thank goodness, it was not the same church where I used to sing in the choir. After church I was allowed to go home for a few minutes, which I did, in the livery and top hat with a cockade. At that time I lost my sweetheart. She said she would not have a flunkey for a sweetheart, besides, I could never get out to see her.

Pray do not think I was resting, although I was in the house in the afternoon. It was a large, new house and the lady was constantly re-arranging the furniture. I had to carry it up and down stairs, try it here, try it there, so that by the time I had to go to bed I was as tired as a dog: she would keep me constantly on. Which reminds me of a little general servant. Some years ago it was compulsory to be vaccinated, through the outbreak of some disease in England. The Doctor was about to vaccinate the girl, when she asked him if she would be able to use her arm to do her work. He replied, "No, you will have to rest your arm." She asked, *"Must* you do it on my arm?—I don't get any time for sitting down," as an afterthought.

When requiring a boy for gentleman's service most employers apply to the clergyman or school-master to see if they have a suitable boy just leaving school that would be suitable for a beginner. They generally select a delicate boy that would crumple up if put to hard outdoor work. Hence one sees the pasty-faced footmen and butlers, when front doors open, the result of the want of fresh air. For my part, I began to feel like a young lion in chains. I missed my games with my schoolmates at evening time.

At the place I was then at they could not keep their servants. I saw three cooks in the short time I was there, the last one, who was shortly to be married, bolted one night, for she could not get away in the daytime, as the old Captain or his wife were always watching. Her fiancée brought her a rope, and came one night. She let her box down out of the bedroom window with the rope: in the morning they found she was gone, box and all.

No one was allowed to come to the house to see the servants. One day my mother sent some clean

linen for me by my little brother. I talked to him
for a few minutes, when I heard the lady coming
down the kitchen stairs. I was frightened. I did
not know what to do, so I popped him in the cupboard where the firewood was kept by the side of
the kitchen fireplace. She asked, "Where is that
boy that came in the gate? We saw him come in,
and have not seen him go out." I said, "He's
gone, Mam." She went back and watched.
When I thought all was safe I let him out, but as
he passed the front door, they both pounced on
and seized him, demanded of him where he had
been. He told them he had been waiting. So he
had: he had been waiting for a chance to get out
of the cupboard. My mother would not let me
remain long in such a place, whose reputation was
not very good in the town, so I left shortly after.
I began to think to myself if this is gentleman's
service I have had enough of it allready.

When I was with the Doctor we often used to
go to a large old-fashioned house about a mile out
of town. The gentleman used to drive his yellow
four-in-hand coach. I was awed when I saw the
pompous butler and two powdered footmen with
red breeches and white silk stockings, come to the
front door, and wonder if I should ever be like they
were. One day I had to take a note there and wait
a reply. The footman took me in, along a broad
passage, opened a door and pushed me in, saying,

"Someone to see you, ladies!" I thought they were ladies, all sitting round the room at needle-work. I found out afterwards it was the house-maids' room.

CHAPTER III

I NOW had to look for another place, and got one from an advertisement in the county newspaper, to go to Eastbourne, about sixty miles from my home, as footman.

I had the usual good advice from my mother, who came to the station to "see me off," accompanied by the straining of heart strings on both sides, as it was my first time of leaving home. The train started, and as the poet sayeth:

"I could lie down like a tired child,
    And weep away this life of care,
    Which I have borne, and yet must bear."

Though I had to work hard I was fairly happy in this place, after my homesickness had worn off. They treated me fairly well. There were children in the family. I had twelve or fourteen pairs of boots to clean before breakfast. There were compensations. When I got out I would go down to the sea and hire a boat, for I could row; also, I found a friend, a footman who lived near. We would go boating and bathing together. One incident that happened there I have not forgotten. On the 5th of November, at Eastbourne, also at Lewes, they used to have a torchlight procession, bonfire, and burn the efigy of the most unpopular person of that time. I got permission to go out, the Master giving me some letters to post. I put on my buff livery overcoat as it was very cold, putting the letters in my pocket. The procession was approaching. Of course, I must join it. I got a torch and lighted it, and marched on with the others. The next time I wanted that overcoat, to go on the carriage as footman, I found it was covered with spots of tar that had fallen from the torch; but this was not all. I felt that there was something in a pocket. I felt: it was the letters I had been given to post, a fortnight before. Now, what was to be done? Burn them? No; that would not be right, as I did not know what they contained. So, with "my tail between my legs," I went up to the study.

The Master did not say much, but the look he gave me, over the top of his spectacles, was enough. He said: "I have been wondering why I did not get these letters answered." In the excitement of the procession I had forgotten to post those letters. At that place I learned to do crochet work, and could beat any girl at making lace and wool work. During my years in service I have made dozens of jackets for babies; in fact, I think the women used to have the babies in order to get the little wool jacket; also, no end of woolen crossovers for old women.

A servant has to stay within hearing of the bells and telephone, and when the other work was finished for the time being, I would crochet. I cannot bear to sit doing nothing but twiddle my thumbs, neither can I bear going for a "walk" without some object in view.

I have often smiled to myself, when I see a photograph taken at the time I was at Eastbourne. What a rig out? A very short frock coat, and a round, flat Scotch cap, perched on a mop of curly hair. I thought at the time I was absolutely "It."

After about two years I thought it time I should make a move, and be getting on, as I was worthier a better place. So I left and went home. I was not there long. It is astonishing what a difference two years make to a town: all my school-mates had gone. Strangers everywhere. I went to see the house where the Doctor lived: strangers there too. I looked at the nick in the wall where I used to put the toe of my boot to climb over when I was late. I thought of the happy times I had spent there, and I think I dropped a tear. No; I did not want to stay at home long.

I soon got a place, as second footman to a Baronet, about forty miles from home, being a tall boy for my age. Now I began to find out what real gentleman's service was. The butler was a decent, old-fashioned sort. Here the beer was drawn in leather jacks, and drank out of horns.

We ate our food off pewter plates.   It was a good, old-fashioned country place: hunting, shooting, fishing was indulged in.   The first footman and I had sixty-three colza oil lamps to clean and trim, before breakfast, after collecting them from all parts of the house.   Her Ladyship, a little old lady, had me in, and talked to me nicely.   We were all happy and comfortable.   About twenty servants were kept.   There was no hurry and scurry like service is now-a-days.   One felt at home.   I was quick to learn.   The butler taught me how to polish silver properly, and all my other duties, and such as running up and down stairs that one cannot see, for the stairs are out of sight when one has a butler's tray full of silver and glass in front of one: it requires a bit of judgment, especially when one thinks they are at the bottom and there is another step to go.   He soon saw he could trust me.   After supper we had dancing in the servants' hall.   I had learnt to play the concertina (an instrument much in vogue in those days) but the sound of which I now detest.   Old rules were kept up, we were not allowed to converse at the servants' hall dinner, untill the "quality," usually called "Pugs" had left the hall, consisting of housekeeper, cook, lady's-maids, valets, butler, formed quite a procession to the steward's room, where they had—well, we were not supposed to know what they had.

One bank holiday, Good Friday, I think it was, my father came to see me unexpectedly. The butler made him welcome. He sat down to dinner with us in the hall, and would keep on talking on general topics, much to the amusement of all the rest of us, and could not understand why no one answered him. I explained to him afterwards.

I was perfectly happy while there. It was the sort of a place one could live at all their days, if contented with a country life—miles from any-where—but we were a little comunity in ourselves.

Nothing pleased me better, when it was my turn off duty, to go and find the gamekeeper and get a shot at a rabbit. On Sundays a large brake came to the side door to take such of the servants who wished to go to church, a drive of three miles across the Downs. I took alternate Sundays with the first footman, always returning with a double-barreled appetite for the twenty-five pounds of roasted ribs of beef at one end of the table, and a boiled leg of mutton and trimmings at the other; followed by large black plum puddings, such as is usually served at Christmas.

While at this place I began the habit of having a cold bath (which I put ready overnight) on jumping out of bed every morning. Often I have had to break the ice on the water before I could begin, our bedrooms were so cold, but we fortified

ourselves against it by making a jack of hot spiced
ale before going to bed in winter.

Unfortunately, after I had been there nearly
two years, her Ladyship died. There was an
enormous funeral: the house was packed with
guests. After all was over, and things had quieted
down a bit, we were told that great alterations and
reductions would take place, as the Baronet was
now alone in the house. About half the servants
got a month's notice to leave, myself among them.
So again I went home.

During my absence my youngest sister had gone
away into service, also my brother had got a page-
boy's place. This is what gentleman's service
does. It scatters and seperates members of a family all over the country. One never knows where
they will have to go next. Perhaps not seeing
each other for years.

So I found my mother all alone, though she had
the consolation of my father coming home from
his work in the evening: that was all. I wandered
round the town, but met scarcely anyone I knew.
All my schoolmates had grown into young men
and young women; some had left the town; some
had got married; and several I knew had died. I
saw the old schoolmaster at his gate. His hair
had turned quite white. His son had turned out
to be a rascal, which helped it a bit, no doubt.
Which goes to show that though he had the best

education, unless the good principle is there, it is of no avail; as witness the verger's son who had, through influence, been educated in the Blue Coat School, where they were supposed to get a better commercial education than we had. On leaving school he got a post as clerk at the railway station. One day he delivered a parcel to my mother, saying there was tenpence to pay. She gave him the money. On opening the parcel she found nothing but a brick and some straws. My mother would always laugh at our boyish escapades, but this was dishonesty. She took no action but told his father what he had done. The meadow next the school was built over, which I looked on as a sacriledge, when I remembered the stolen games of cricket we used to play there. The cricket ground, where the County teams used to play, was all cut up with roads, and covered with villas. Everything about the place seemed so small. I went and hired a boat a few times, dug up the garden, but soon got tired of being about, where everything was so different to what it was when I left home.

I had kept up a desultory correspondence with the footman who I lived with at the Doctor's, and who was now a butler in London. I wrote to him. He strongly advised me to come to London, where he would quickly get me a situation. We talked the matter over, and I decided to go. I shall never forget the morning I started. My father got half

a day to see me off and came to the station.   When
the train was about to start, he actually kissed me.
That was the last time I ever saw him in a state
of consciousness, for the next time I saw him he
was on his death-bed.

As the train neared London I began to wonder
how I should find my way in such a maze of houses
and streets.   But one need never get lost, as long
as one has a tongue: so by constant enquiry I
found my way from Waterloo Station to Belgrave
Square.

I arrived in London to seek my fortune.   Not
with the proverbial half-a-crown in my pocket, for
I think I had a little more than that, but not much.
I found my friend.   He had found lodgings for
me in some mews quite handy.   I was no longer
home sick, only a bit confused at the size of London.   Still, I meant to push my way onward and
upward.   We scanned the advertisements for
servants.   I forget to mention that I arrived in
London wearing a straw hat with a cerice ribbon
round it, thinking it was quite smart, but my
friend, the butler, told me that it was not the right
thing at all for London wear; so I struck my colours, and put on a black ribbon.

It is curious how a single letter in the alphabet
may alter the whole course of one's life.   In an
advertisement it stated that a footman was wanted
in Walton Street, whereas it was in Wilton Street

that the footman was wanted; by the time I had been to Walton Street (someone suggested it meant "Wilton") and back to Wilton Street, I was too late, the place had just been taken.

On occasions when scouring the West End of London in search of a situation often I could not afford to have a cookshop dinner, but would go to a baker's shop and buy a twopenny loaf, also a quarter of a pound of cheese, take it to some isolated part of the Green Park, or Hyde Park, and eat it.

On one of these occasions I was lunching on one of the seats in Chelsea Churchyard, when a poor looking man came towards me. I thought to myself, "I suppose the poor fellow is hungry." He did not ask for anything, but remarked, "It's a very keen wind!" I said it was, and asked him if he had dined, if not, that he was welcome to some of mine. "No," he said, "I have some cabbage on cooking now." "Only cabbage?" I asked. "Just cabbage," he replied. "But God is my other satisfying portion. He satisfieth me. And God expects the very best that is in us, nothing shoddy, half-hearted, but the very best." He got up and went away. I fancy he must have been a tailor in a small way, living in one of the small cottages near the Churchyard.

At this time I found myself a strong, healthy young man. Height, 5 feet 8 inches. Quick to take offence, but quicker to forgive. I only hoped that I should continue to grow, so as to enable me to serve in some of the highest families in the land. For, in those days, footmen in good families had to be not less than six feet, and taller if possible, to show off the family livery, and look important. "Swank."

There is a great difference in boys. Some are adaptable to be trained for service, some are too slow and dull, others are sharp. I have trained several in my time, to be, I believe, good servants, but as to whether they have lived to thank, or curse, me for doing so, is a question.

When I first came to London, in my spare time, when I was not actually looking for a place, I tried to learn my way about. I got a map and would sally forth; sometimes I got lost, but one can always ask the way. Thus I learnt most of the West End of London. One day I started to see the Tower—before I got the map—after I had followed the river Thames for an hour or so, thinking that would surely bring me to it, I found I had gone the wrong way altogether, and found myself at Hammersmith.

I soon got a place as second footman in a large place in ——shire, with a Nobleman, who I call "The Bold Bad Baron," for he was the surliest, bad-tempered man I ever met. Here they kept twenty-five indoor servants. We had to powder,

and wear breeches and white stockings. The
livery was green, covered with yellow and black
brading, the family crest being worked in the
brade. The under butler previously had valeted
his Lordship, but he gave notice to leave, so they
offered him the post as under butler, if he would
stay on. He took it, and the valeting of his Lordship fell to me, and well I knew it: a galley slave
could not have been treated worse than I was. I
soon understood why the under butler wanted to
leave. The butler was a pompous sort of a man,
though a very good sort. He had previously
served the Rothschilds. As long as we did our
work properly he would not trouble us, in fact he
very seldom spoke to us liverymen.

The house was very large, an old Elizabethan
mansion, partly modernised inside, but in the
rooms upstairs Moderator colza oil lamps were
used, and wax candles; gas was used in the basement, made on the estate; the passages were so
wide a horse and cart could easily go up them.
These passages all met in a large stone flagged
square, so that it took some time to find the way
about.

It was then the fashion for gentlemen to part
their hair in the centre at the back of the head.
I had to do this for the Baron, he would then take
the handglass, and say that it was not a straight
parting, or that I had put more hair one side than

the other, and I had to do it all over again, he moving his head about, and using some very flowery language. But I was as full of life as an egg, and free from care. The Baron's bad language was like water on a duck's back: it did not soak in; but after a time came to be a bit monotinous. Being miles from anywhere what amusements we had we had to make ourselves.

There was a goodly company of us in the servants' hall at night, as the grooms and the under-gardeners would come in, and wash up all the silver and glass in the pantries; more for company than anything else, for there was nowhere for them to go for miles, in the evenings. So that by the time we had finished waiting dinner, all the glass and silver would be washed up and put away: all we had to do was to adjourn to supper. There was the usual old-fashioned usages observed in the servants' hall, such as drinking the "Health" every day, etc., also a certain amount of "Esprit de Corps" among us all, which at the present day is entirely absent. I shall never forget one day. The head laundry-maid took my face between her hands and kissed me before them all, said she could not resist it. She was a woman of forty, stout and buxom, and I a chubby boy of eighteen, though I went as aged twenty. I also went crimson. I think it was one day that I had got an extra whigging from the "Bold Bad Baron," so she kissed it all away for me: for they all knew what sort of a man he was. But it would take more than that to make me blush now-a-days.

The housekeepers in those days wore a black silk dress, a little silk apron trimmed with beads, a lace collar, and a large gold brooch, a small apology for a cap, made of white lace, and a black velvet bow on top. The under-maids were more afraid of her than they were of her Ladyship.

On Sundays the maids had all to troop off to church, which was in the grounds, and had to wear small black bonnets, with ribbons tied in a bow under the chin, similar to bonnets worn by nurses. The pews for the servants were opposite to those of the gentry, so that we were under observation all the time. One Sunday the Bold Bad Baron sent for the butler after church and asked him if we had been drinking too much beer as he noticed several of the men servants were asleep during the sermon. The parson was brother to the Baron, the living was in his gift, so of course he preached a sermon to please him; generally about the lower orders being submissive to their betters. Servants to be obedient to their masters, and satisfied to be jumped on and trodden down generally. No wonder we went to sleep. Still, we managed to be fairly happy amongst ourselves, though there was plenty of work for everybody. At this time I discarded the concertina, and started to learn to

play the violin. Some people say I play well,
and could get my living at it; at any rate, I know
I play with expression.

The first footman was a dare-devil, in disposition similar to the footman I lived with at the
Doctor's in my first place. He would glory in
any sort of mischief, especially in tormenting the
under butler. All the men slept in the basement.
The under butler let his bed down in the pantry,
across the front of the plate room door, so as to
guard the plate at night. To get at it, burglars
would have to move his bed: if that did not waken
him nothing would. I was supposed to sleep at
the porter's lodge, down two hundred yards of
passage, where two grooms and the usher slept,
but I could not hear his Lordship's bell so far
away, so by arrangement with the first footman
we changed bedrooms. One night we arranged to
have a game with the under butler, so we got a
reel of cotton, put it on top of his let-down bed,
taking the end of the cotton down the passage
round the next corner with us. When we saw
him put out his light we gently began to pull the
cotton. We heard him get out of bed, strike a
light to see what it was rattling on the top of his
bed. Then we thought it prudent to disappear to
our own rooms in stockinged feet. Another night
we tied a string to the corner of his bedclothes,

waited till we thought he had gone to sleep, then we began gently to pull his bedclothes off. But he had not gone to sleep, but had discovered the plot, and was waiting for us with the wooden bar that kept his bed up in the day time. He shot out after us, and laid on with the bar. We all being in our nightshirts, the bar fitted pretty close to the part we generally sit on, but it was all taken in good part; but as we had to pass the butler's door we dare not cry out, or make a noise. After "Lights Out," the secretary, who slept in his quarters near the porter's lodge, would go into the butler's room, about midway down the passage, to have a chat, and doubtless tap a bottle of the best.

One night, after "Lights Out," we arranged to go to the porter's lodge to have a game of cards, generally brag or nap. We did not notice the flight of time. Suddenly we heard the butler and secretary coming down the passage, the butler to see that the back entrance was bolted, the secretary to go to bed.

Immediately the gas was turned out, as a window looked out on the passage. The under butler got under one of the beds. He was rather a stout chap, and inclined to "embompoint," the first footman and I got into the bed and pulled the clothes up over our heads. The under butler groaned out, "Get off, get off, you're squeezing me to death."

Our weight had made the bed go down and so pinched him; the others had hid themselves as best they could, in cupboards, anywhere, and were as quiet as mice. There was only one door: that led out to where the butler stood. He stood there a second or two, apparently listening, then went on. What would have happened if he had opened the door, goodness knows. A pretty picture he would have seen. Two footmen in bed with their livery and powdered hair, and the under butler's white stockinged legs sticking out from under the bed. For in those days butlers were butlers. We had to say, "Yes, sir," and "No, sir," when he spoke to us, which was not very often; and when he told us to do anything we had to jump to it quick. When all was quiet, we all crept up the passage, a little light came through the lights in the roof (which was a garden terrace outside). When we had got fifty yards up, and nearly opposite the butler's door, he locked it: we thought he was opening it, so all turned tail; in the retreat I caught my forehead against a projecting part of the wall and had a lovely big bump there next day. I also dropped one of my pumps I was carrying. After a time we tried again, and got through successfully. All this fun helped to neutralise the bullyings and jawings I got from the Bold Bad Baron when valeting him. He seemed to meet everything "edge on," all his money and power did not make him happy; his wife and family were afraid of him whenever he appeared on the scene; the scowl on his face never left him: no doubt it was there when he died.

CHAPTER IV

THE under butler was very fond of a grilled bone
for tea. (The chef would average out the weight
of meat according to the number of servants, and
the bones never went back to the kitchen, except
at Sunday dinner, when the cold beef came in
again for supper.) He would lay a shoulder of
mutton bone on the bright wood ashes of the fire,
then pick it: no wonder he got so fat. One day
he put it on his plate, and turned to get the pepper
and salt. I made a grab for the bone, but he was
too quick for me. I made a bolt for the door.
He flung the bone at me, it stuck in the plaster
of the wall, four inches, by the shank end, and
stood straight out. Had it struck the back of my
head, which it missed by a few inches, What Ho!

The maidservants only came into the servants'
hall for dinner and supper, their other meals they
got in their own apartments, the kitchen maids
never came, except when a dance was on. The
laundry maids in the laundry, the housemaids in
housemaids' room; the dairy maid would feed with
the stillroom maids; nursemaids in their nursery;
butler, valets, groom of chambers, housekeeper,
lady's-maids in the steward's room. So that there

is a lot of one servant waiting on another, the under ones of each department doing it, they in turn being waited on, when promoted.

In cases when visitors were staying in the house we wore our dress liveries, with a lot more yellow and black brade plastered up the back and across the front. The butler wore black cloth breeches and black silk stockings. Our silver shoe buckles were on the plate list, and had to be given up when leaving the situation. The Bold Bad Baron gave a ball each year, as he held a high position in the County, besides that, he had a daughter he wanted to get "off." The family went away for a week before the ball, in order that the servants should prepare and have everything "spick and span." The butler set us to do all sorts of odd jobs. The Baronial Hall was used as the ball room. It was about thirty yards long by twenty-five yards wide, with a minstrel gallery at one end. A two-foot shelf ran round level with the minstrel gallery, on which were old blue jars and other curios, about twelve feet from the polished oak floor. The butler set me to dust and polish this shelf, as the housemaids could not do it. I got a ladder and set to work: the ladder slipped away at the bottom. I managed to grip the edge of the shelf: there I hung. I shouted, someone came and pushed up the ladder (I could not have held on another minute), and so saved me from getting a decent bump on the hard floor. After that I got a half-hundredweight and put it at the foot of the ladder. I could see no fear in those days. A similar thing happened a few days afterwards. The Baron told me to clean his dressing room windows while he was away. The first footman and I went to the farm and got a long ladder, as I found that two of the windows did not open, so had to be cleaned from the outside. We had some rare fun sliding the ladder over the deep snow, on inclines we got on and had a ride. Eventually we got the ladder reared up. I did the outsides, standing on the window sill. To my horror, the ladder slipped away on the frosty ground at the bottom: I had no escape. I shouted to the first footman inside the room and told him what had happened. He had a long way to go to get to the foot of the ladder to push it up. I was left hanging on by an inch of window frame, on a slippery, icy window-sill: it seemed hours. I was up thirty feet. At last he appeared, and pushed up, and held the ladder. I tremblingly crept down and said, "Never again."

Our chef was a decent little fellow. He was a son of a very eminent chef in London at the time. He was very fair to all the other servants as regards their food. There is a great deal of difference in chefs in this respect. One, in Grosvenor Place, I lived with would not give the servants

enough food; when I complained, after speaking
to him, and no improvement, he told the lady:
"Zey have eggs and bacon and sausages for breakfast." We did, but a little piece of bacon each
one morning, a fried egg each the next, and a tiny
sausage the next, other meals in proportion. But
I noticed he always had a parcel when he went
home at night on his bicycle to Soho where he had
a large family to feed.

Another chef, an Italian, came at me with a
long knife because a footman had put the kettle
for the drawing room tea on the kitchen hotplate
to boil: it was in the summer time, and no other
fires in the house. I thought he was going to
"knife me," shouting, "Make your own fires," like
a madman. Gentry are always partial to foreign
servants: they will chatter to them for a length of
time, whereas, if it is a British servant, it is, go and
get on with your work, "you dirty dog" sort of air.
I think it is mostly to keep their foreign conversation from getting rusty, but no one can tell what
they are talking about. I consider it very bad
manners for a conversation to be carried on at the
table by foreign servants, which the others cannot
understand. But our chef at the Baron's was not
of that sort: he was a jolly fellow. He had a trick
of bringing a pot of good soup to the pantry on
a cold winter's morning at eleven o'clock, exchang-
ing it for our beer. (I wonder what makes kit-

chen people so thirsty? I suppose it is the fires.)

One day he came rushing to the pantry with all his hair, moustache, and eyebrows burnt off. It appeared one of the kitchen maids had turned off the gas in one of the ovens, and turned it on again, then shut the door. The chef went to light the gas some time after, with a taper, hence explosion and hair off, but it soon grew again. We could not help roaring with laughter, he did look comical, though it might have been serious.

The ball came off in due course: it made everybody busy: extra waiters were got in: a horseshoe shaped buffet was rigged up in the dining room, leading off the Baronial Hall. Two footmen were on duty at the front door, and no lack of help behind the scenes. When all was ready the guests began to arrive, besides having a house full. I had three extra to valet. One morning something went wrong with one of the blinds, when I was calling one of them, so I went to get a pair of steps to put it right. I went towards the window, and happened to look at the bed. There lay a young lady, apparently asleep. I had gone into the wrong room. I quickly and quietly took the steps out. It is difficult to know the rooms in a long corridor, especially if they have no names or numbers. I heard nothing of it, though I looked at the young lady when at dinner, to see if there was any sign of recognition.

On another morning, at another time, I was taking a can of hot shaving water to a gentleman. I opened the door after knocking: there stood a lady in a flat bath, her back was towards me. I quietly shut the door. The splash of the water prevented her from hearing me knock. Besides, she should have bolted the door. I thought to myself: "This is no place for Curates, and I so young too: a jolly good thing she was not facing a mirror, or she would have seen me, and I should have lost my eyesight, and probably my place as well." People were more modest in those days, but now the ladies don't seem to care if they are seen with scanty clothing, or even none at all. In fact I have been interviewed by ladies in bed on two occasions lately, when trying for a situation. One would imagine that the fact of the gentry having more money, without work, commanding the best of everything the world produces, would tend to develop and bring out everything that is pure and good in human nature. But it does not. Every day there is evidence of "Anyone's wife but their own: and anyone's husband but their own," they soon tire of each other.

But let us get on with the mazy dance. Although we had been hard at work since the early morning, as soon as the band struck up it seemed to put new life into us. The first footman and I were taken from the front door to help in the buffet, and one thing we dare not forget was to go round every two hours and wind up the moderator colza oil lamps, also watch the candles burning, to see if they required replacing, clearing up any stray wine glasses, etc., that may have got into the ball room. The Baron was fond of pomp and show, and liked to see his dress liveries walking about. About four o'clock in the morning it was all over. Then the clearing up began: by the time that was done it was time to begin the ordinary day's work, after we had changed our clothes. This is where that patent handle is wanted to wind servants up, to work on again for another fifteen hours; anyhow, we had to do it, no going to bed, and there is no over-time pay for servants, as in other trades. But I thought of those lines:—

"We pray you, kind and gentle guest,
    For mercy's sake, let's have a rest,
    And may your guiding spirits lead you
    Homeward bound, and quickly speed you."

What wonder, then, when we saw a chance of a little relaxation and fun we took it. One Sunday afternoon the under butler and I, being off duty, got up a party of the servants, not forgetting the buxom head laundry maid, for a punting party on the lake in the park. All was ready, the maids occupying the stern of the punt; we pushed off, and to our consternation, the stern of the punt, being overloaded, went under water. There was a terrible scrabble to get the maids out of the water, with all their Sunday clothes spoilt, and covered with green weeds. The head laundry-maid did not kiss me on that occasion. But our final escapade came later on.

.   .   .   .

As the London season came round, we packed up, and went to town. On going out to dinner, or other function, the Baron always had two footmen standing up behind his C spring carriage, and the coachman with his curly wig on. The Baron was a big bug at his seat in the country, but when he got to London, among other big bugs, he was not such a very big bug after all. A London season is very tiring to servants. There is not only the day work, but the night work as well. They would keep us out regularly till one, two, or three o'clock, but we had to start work at the same time as the other servants.

Often during the London season we were kept so short of our hours of sleep that I used to go to sleep on the carriage; the coachman would notice it and draw the handle of his knotty whip under my nose. I would wake up with a start, and wonder where I was.

One footman, who lived near us in the country, went to sleep on the box of a high barouche, and actually fell backwards, and landed among the ladies. Of course they would say he was tipsy, or "Tishy."

It is useless trying to describe the thousand and one things that comprise a footman's duties, which, in every place he goes to, is different. It is like throwing a stone in a pond, rings are formed in the water, which eventually fades quite away. So that at the end of his day's work he can show nothing that he has done. He has made nothing, produced nothing, yet he has been constantly on the alert all day, not knowing where his next job will spring from. It may be a ring at the front door, to take some dressmaker's boxes to the lady's-maid at the top of the house, and bring down the empty boxes. While he had been upstairs perhaps his master or mistress has rung the front door bell, and has been kept waiting. They demand to know "why" in no very pleasant tone of voice.

Sometimes two or three jobs will spring up, all wanting to be done at the same time. Even to scrubbing a pound's worth of silver coins; for who knows what germs may be on them after they have been handled by the common working classes.

We were all glad to get back to the country house again after the London season, with its dinner parties, tea parties, evening parties and night work. Things went on fairly quiet till the garden parties came on, and the house began to fill up with visitors. This is the time to do the duty entertaining of poor relations, who come with a handbag, and go away with two dress baskets. But, poor things, they can't help being poor, and taking away the things that the ladies' maids and valets ought to have. Apropos of this sort of thing happened in a small place only a short time ago in the country, where only two maids were kept. In the good old days it was the custom when visitors who had stayed perhaps a week or so, for them to give the servants a tip, just to show they appreciated the services rendered them, and to compensate the servants for the extra work they had caused. It was usual for them to put the tip for the housemaids under the pillow of the bed. We had a very smart footman who knew this. As soon as the visitors left their bedrooms on the last morning of their visit he used to pop round the bedrooms and take the tip from under the pillows, and then disappear downstairs. He was seen to come out of the bedrooms, where he had no business to be, and as there was never any tips for the housemaids while he had been there, the butler was told, who laid a trap for him, by putting a marked half sovereign under the pillow. Sure enough he fell into the trap. When he came downstairs the butler told him to turn out his pockets. He had the marked coin and the sack as well.   But servants do not have to worry much about tips now-a-days.   The gentry want some-one to give them a tip.   When they leave by the front door after a visit, the servants have so shrunken in size that they can't see them, and it is always those visitors who give the servants most trouble that give the smallest or no tip at all.

In the past a gentleman and his wife had been visiting the house for a few days.   When they left in a car they left nothing behind them for the servant.   They started, but suddenly remembered the fact, so stopped, and sent the chauffeur back with a ten shilling note for the servant.   She not being at the door, he gave it to the lady, who was there.   The lady gave the servant five shillings as from them; and two half-crowns as coming from two of her poor relations when they went away shortly after.   Another curious thing happened while we were in Buckinghamshire, worth relating. I have no animosity against the church, being a church-goer myself, when I get the chance.   As, without a doubt, there is something in all human beings, rich or poor, that one cannot smother; will not be trampled down.   Live a life of a beast, a fish, a drunkard if you will, but it will always crop up, even against your will.   It is your Conscience. "As a man, or woman sows, so shall they reap." Though a great many reaps where they have not sown.

Everyone of us have our own standard of what is right: but on its being boiled down, and analised, proves to be selfish every time. I consider it a greater sin for a rich man to withhold help and assistance to the poor, or a person that really wants to get on in the world honestly, than for a starving person to steal bread, meat, or a rabbit off his land. "Oh," the rich exclaim, "but I subscribe to this and that charity, you can see my name in the papers that I do it," but that is not the thing. Most of these charities are sifted through a ladder, that which remains on the ladder goes to charity. That which goes through the ladder goes to the management. I have never met anyone that has benefitted by them individually. Neither is it charity in the true sence of the word when one sees So-and-So died, leaving £10,000 to such a charity or hospital. He or she held the money to the very last gasp of breath in their bodies; if they had lived another five years so would they have held on to the money that five years, and if possible, would have taken it with them. It is no true charity to give away something that cannot possibly be of any use to you.

. . . .

Now for the story about the parson.

Those servants that could be spared used to trip off down to the villiage church on Sundays. The schoolmistress played the harmonium: she being a nice person the servants got acquainted with her, and asked her to come to tea at the "big house." The parson and his wife also came up to lunch. They were about to have a jumble sale in the schoolroom. The outcome of it was: I and the ladies maid had to pack two large laundry hampers full of clothes, which the Bos and Mistress turned out. I had to take them down to the parson's house. On arriving, he came to the door, we took the hampers in. I said: "I beg pardon, Sir, but I packed two pairs of dark trowsers that would be of great use to me. If you will state a price, I would like to have them, and will pay for them now." "Oh, no," he replied, "We do not do things that way." I said, "I'm sorry. Hope no offence."

The schoolmistress was to be behind the counter at the sale, so I went to her, described the trowsers, gave her the money to pay for them, asking her to seize them as soon as the sale was opened. On going for them the next day she said there were no trowsers at the sale. The parson had two grown-up sons of his own; so the trowsers never reached the sale room at all.

Although we used to make what amusements we could amongst ourselves, I felt that I was gradually going into a net, and losing all liberty in life: the constraint became almost unbearable, but what could I do? I had no trade in my hands.

I knew nothing but gentleman's service wherewith to get a living. I suppose some men does not feel it, men with no further ambition than to fritter their lives away from day to day in such a calling; a sort of man-woman existance, at the mercy of the gentry's whims and fancies; cooped up day and night, without variation. But Fate, or something we did, shortly brought a change.

One night, after "lights out" upstairs, and we had all finished work for that day; by chance we were all going down the passage to our various rooms, we all branched off to my room on the right, at the foot of a back staircase. There was the under butler, first footman, two under gardeners, two grooms, and myself. We began larking about, at one thing and another, and making more noise than we thought. We were too far away from the butler's room for him to hear us. Anyhow, it ended up with a pillow fight. Just as the end of one of the pillows burst, and the feathers flew all over the room, the door opened, and there stood the Bold Bad Baron, with a silver candle-stick in his hand. I suppose as he was going to bed, passing the top of the staircase, he heard the scrimmage going on, and came down to see what it was. We looked pretty with our hair powder knocked off by the pillows. I think it was knocking each other's powder off that began the meleè. His Lordship said: "Whose room is this?" I said: "Mine, my Lord." He said: "I will see you all at ten o'clock to-morrow morning." Next morning we were all ranged up in the library wondering what was to happen next. His Lordship came in at the door opposite, looking as black as thunder. The outcome of it all was: the under-butler was severely cautioned, and told he ought to know better, the first footman got the sack, I was cautioned as to my future conduct, the two under gardeners were forbidden to come into the house, so for the future they would have to keep each other company in their little bothy in the garden. No doubt the butler got a whigging, and told he could not manage his men, or something of that sort. I was sorry for him, for as long as we did our work properly, he never interfered with us. He simply gave each of us our orders in the morning and we executed them. But a sence of depression seemed to come over the place; so after things had quieted down, I sent in a month's notice to leave. On leaving I received a telegram to say my father had met with an accident while at work, and that I was to go home at once; but by the time I got there he was dead. It appears a heavy load from a crane had fallen on him, crushing him so that his ribs were broken and driven into his lungs: he bled to death internally. All this time that I had been away in service I always sent the greater part of my wages home, but in those days, a second footman got £28 a year, and had to pay his own laundry bill out of that. We were allowed £2 per year for hair powder, but always used flour. There was no such thing as Employers' Liability in those days, so we got nothing except the £12 from the Foresters' Club, which my father belonged to. Enough to pay funeral expences and a little over. After the funeral, which was attended by all his fellow-workmen, my mother and the rest of the family talked things over, as to ways and means for the future. My eldest sister was married, and lived in the Isle of Wight, my youngest sister in service, lived near her. It was decided my youngest brother should leave his place in service, and come home to live with mother, who otherwise would be all alone. The undertaker promised to give him work in oak carving, and being a clever fellow in most things he made rapid progress. He was also a good musician, and joined the County Regiment Volunteer Band. At meal times he took his cornet, blowing it (so as to learn marching and playing at the same time) to and from his meals, much to the amusement of the neighbours. He also learnt to play the violin.

During the time I was at home a certain General, living not far away, sent for me to know if I would go and assist, as he was giving a garden party, he having two daughters he wanted to get "off." I went, and found it was a lively affair.

Boat loads of officers rowed up from the Men o'
War ships in Portsmouth harbour. There was a
military band and lots of officers from the forts
and barracks. After it was over some of the officers lingered behind. The gardener and one of
the boat's crew proposed to have a bathe: no
sooner said than done. We jumped into the Man
o' War's boat, and pulled out to the middle. The
gardener and the sailor were good swimmers: I
never was very good at it for a long distance. We
were soon stripped, and overboard they went, the
sailor put the painter round his neck and pulled
the boat along. I, not liking to show the "white
feather," dived overboard too. By the time I
came to the surface I found the boat had got a
length or two ahead of me. I put on a spurt, but
it was as much as I could do to keep pace with
them, and soon began to tire, so decided to make
another effort and get into the boat. When alongside, I made a grab for the gunwale, missed, and
went under the boat. When I came up I found
the boat had got several lengths ahead. I would
not call out, though nearly exhausted, but made
another spurt. This time, I thought, I will make
no mistake. I just caught the gunwale with my
fingers, but my body was sucked under the boat.
I hung on, and gradually got a better hold, drawing my body up, also drawing a lot of skin off my
ribs, which the salt water tingled up nicely. I

thought to myself, "That's the second near squeak of being drowned. I wonder what the next will be like?" But that came later in Scotland.

Now we had to begin to think about ways and means at home. We decided to let two rooms for lodgings, to a man and woman, who paid at first, but after getting in arrears with their rent, "hopped it" one night without paying, besides taking some of our things with them. Soon after this my youngest sister got married to a fellow who turned out to be a "waster." He was full of promices, and bragged of what he could do. He took a provision shop in London, but failed, through inattention to the business. He got into debt, and did a "Moonlight flit" one night. But my sister had great faith, and clung to him like the ivy, "The greater the ruin, the tighter it clings."

CHAPTER V

As there was no suitable work round about there, near home, for me—as, after being in large places I would not go into a small one—I determined to go back to London, and try my fortunes there. On arrival I found lodgings, the same place I had before, near Belgrave Square, on the first occasion of my coming to London. To my consternation I found that I had stopped growing, at five feet nine inches: and had broadened out, not flabily, but firmly. My chest measure was forty inches, waist forty inches, arm muscles sixteen and a half, neck the same, calf of leg the same, and as strong and healthy as a young bull. So I thought, "It's good bye to all thoughts of ever being the King's butler." I had heard that the King's Household was governed by almost military control, so I did not have many regrets on that point: it sounded of red tape.

I also heard at the time, when King Edward was Prince of Wales, it was usual for him to go and see the servants' Christmas dinner laid out. He met a boy with a Christmas pudding, the boy was carrying it up the corridor on his head, saying "God bless the Queen for this enormous Christmas pudding." The Prince said, "That's all right, my boy, but carry the dish in a proper manner." I have waited on, and conversed with, both our present reigning Majesties, but more of that later on.

Now here were two young fellows, my brother and I, who could have done with a "leg up" in the world. Full of life, strength and energy, determined to get on; but money: we had very little of that comodity. As for a "leg up," we might whistle for that till we were tired, or thirsty. My mother had got too old to go out to work. Still, the home had to be kept together somehow. Charity we would not accept, though none was offered from any quarter. I myself have lent friends money when they were down, saying, "If you make good pay me back, but if not don't trouble about it."

I looked round for a place on my arrival in town but to see the servants at the registry offices, waiting to be hired, all looking so meek and humble, filled me with a sence of nausea. I did not feel meek and humble by a long chalk, but more inclined to rebel against it all.

One day I was passing a large railway station in the West End, I wondered if they could offer me any suitable employment. Nothing in the clerk line without experience in railway matters was available, all they had to offer was a porter's job, in corduroys. I thought the matter over, weighed

this and that. I should certainly get more liberty
in life than being a servant. But the rough, dirty
work? The poor food. Well, I knew what that
was when I was a boy. So I said, "All right, sir.
I'll take the job."

I easily produced the references as to character,
without troubling the Bold Bad Baron, and started
work. The shifts were of eight hours each, from
6 A. M. to 2 P. M. from 2 P. M. to 10 P. M. from
10 P. M. to 6 A. M. When off duty I had a sense of
freedom that did my heart good, when compared
to gentleman's service. Night duty consisted of
sweeping out trains, the rest was platform duty,
except once a month two of us were told off to
couple the engines on to the trains as the engines
came back; dirty work, and a bit dangerous. I
was happy enough, though dirty and oily. One
day the head porter called me to take a guard's
van off a train to the yard. I suppose for repairs
or something, but that did not concern me. I
stood ready to couple on the engine when it came
back. I rested my left arm on the buffer, as the
signal was against the engine coming back. The
head porter shouted, "Look out." I had not
noticed the engine creeping back. I naturally
dropped my arm off the buffer just in time for my
elbow to be caught between the two buffers. It is
usual if you shout for the engine driver to put on
steam and back further, thinking I could not get

the link over the hook.   Had he done so my arm
would have been crushed to a jelly.   But the head
porter saw what had happened, and signalled to
the engine driver to go forward.   He made no
mistake.   My arm dropped down.   I managed to
get the coupling on, and get up on to the platform.
I jumped into the van, and then the pain began.
Doubtless the reader has seen a worm squirm when
trodden on in a garden path.   Well, that's how I
squirmed in the guard's van.   I rolled in agony on
the floor of the van.   I took no heed as to where
we were going.   After a time I rolled up my
sleeve.   Two rivet holes pierced my elbow, half an
inch deep, but as I could raise my arm I concluded
no bones were broken, only crushed.   Next day
my arm was very stiff, but I said nothing, and
managed to do my work.   Probably it was noticed
I was a cut above the common, as often I was sent
on local trains as rear guard.   I knew little of this
work at first, and often the engine driver had to
whistle for the brakes to be put on to prevent the
train from running past the stations, but I soon
got to learn and watch for a certain mark, such as
a tall chimney, a particular house, before the train
got into the stations.   One day, when at a City
station, I was speaking to a porter about some
luggage or something, I looked round and saw
my train going out of the station, it looked as
though I was going to be left behind.   I put on

a spurt and just caught an iron rod as the train got to the end of the platform and on to the bridge crossing the Thames. There was not enough room between the train and the bridge for me to open the door of the guard's van. I hung on, but had there been any projection on the bridge I was bound to be swept off; sometimes it was a very close shave, but I flattened myself against the van wondering if I should get caught or not. After we got over the bridge I worked my way along the footboard and into the van. My chums used to say, "Here's the next one to get the guard's clothes." I thought I was getting on all right, when one day I was told to go to the station master's office. He told me he had to send a porter to an out of the way station in the country, and as I was one of the last men taken on he was going to send me. "Well," I thought, "this is rotten, to go to a place where there were perhaps two lots of luggage to handle in a day, miles away from anywhere. That won't suit me." So I immediately gave a week's notice to leave. So, as it was not much use sending me there for one week, he sent some other porter. "This is a little bit of all right," thinks I, "out on the stony rocks again." Here endeth my railway experiences.

It is said a rolling stone gathers no moss; but it gets most devilishly well polished, and I don't think there were any flies on me. I was down,

but I was not out. The more I met adversity, the
fiercer I was to overcome it. I hated the thought
of gentleman's service, but that was the only game
I knew to play properly. Every day I cast round,
studying advertisements, and walking miles, but
found nothing suitable that I could do that would
produce a living wage. So I said to myself,
"Well, my man, it's gentleman's service or starve."
So I cut out the railway episode and asked the
Bold Bad Baron for a reference. I felt that I
would rather go as under butler in a first-class
place, than as first footman in a second-class place;
and I knew the trick of polishing and frosting
silver, which is quite different from simply cleaning it. It was not long before I met with an under
butler's place to a Noble Earl, who had a house in
London, in the country, and one in Scotland. It
requires great strength to polish silver, also great
care and endurance. An under butler is generally
a strong man, and I *was* strong at that time. It
does not matter about his being two or three inches
shorter than the footmen, as he does not appear
at the "front" till late dinner. Here our livery
was very smart. Scarlet breeches and waistcoat,
blue coat with scarlet collar and cuffs, trimmed
with inch wide silver lace, and one epaulet on the
left shoulder, white stockings, and buckles. There
were twenty-five indoor servants at this place, besides housemaids at the other houses. The butler

did no manual work, he only superintended the men, the work was all done for him.   All he had to do was to walk into the dining room, the boy carrying his wine basket, at the last minute, cast his eye over the table, when all was ready to begin. But he was a rotter to his men under him.   Very ignorant, one could scarcely read his writing, and as to arithmatic, he was hopeless.   He thought it lowering to his dignity to speak to an under servant, in fact he seldom did unless it was to give his orders.   He was not good to his wife and children.   He had a good house in the village.   But he had his downfall.   It was his height, being six feet, that kept him where he was.   His downfall was caused by backing slow horses and fast women. This place was the best regulated situation that I have ever been in, and I have either lived in, or visited, when I was a valet, some dozens of the best houses in the kingdom.

When the bell rang to clear breakfast, the butler would answer it.   Her Ladyship was the sister of a Duke.   She would remain in the breakfast room, give the butler his orders for the day, how many visitors (if any) and which rooms they would occupy, the number that would be at meals, also orders for the carriages.   Then he would come out, and the housekeeper would go in and get her orders, she would come out and the cook would go in.   Then the butler would ring the bell twice

for the footman to clear away breakfast.   All this
only took a few minutes to do.   The butler would
come to the pantry and give us our orders.   Perhaps he would say to me, Eighteen, or twenty, for
dinner, use the silver, or the gilt service, as the
case may be.   I had to see to the rest.   To the
footmen he gave orders as to the carriages: and
when addressing him we had to say "Sir"—and
don't forget it.   The housekeeper would give her
orders to the head housemaid, and stillroom maids.
The cook would do the same to her kitchen and
scullerymaids.   Everything went like clockwork,
no confusion, no jealousies, no treading on each
other's toes; no occasion for saying I didn't know
this or that; for each department got their orders,
and acted up to them.   The Castle was a fine old
place, with a wide moat, with water about five feet
deep all round it; the depth of the water could be
increased, by stopping the outlet, to ten feet.   The
place was beseiged by Oliver Cromwell, who left
his marks on it, and some leaden bullets still remain in the front door; a portcullis; and three
drawbridges, two of which were pulled up by the
footmen when closing the house at dark.   The
bridge to the servants' quarters was a fixture.
Inside the front door were holes in the roof, or
ceiling, where boiling pitch would be poured on
the enemy, should he gain an entry.   Suits of old
armour, pikes, swords, muskets, pistols, were in

profusion. The Earl was a fine specimen of an English gentleman; he was well over six feet in height, and broad shouldered. He kept his own pack of foxhounds, and we brewed our own beer in March and October. Everyone who knew the Earl liked and respected him, for he was fair and just in his dealings with everybody. One evening a footman forgot to put the chain across, before he drew up the bridge—he did not know his Lordship was out. His Lordship dropped into the moat in his hunting kit.

Often have I sat up all night with "Old Daddy" as we used to call him. He had brewed the beer for the Castle for over fifty years, and listen to his tales of olden times, of what they used to do in the previous lords time. Still, a great many of the old customs were kept up; we still ate our food off pewter plates and dishes, each with the coronet and crest engraved on them, we also drank our beer out of horns. We had the choice of small beer or tea for breakfast (as tea on its first introduction into England was a guinea a pound, and was used only by the gentry). Also, no conversation was allowed untill after the cloth had been removed, and the health drank. The under butler stands up at the bottom of the table, holds a horn of old ale up in his hands, taps the table twice, and says, "My Lord and Lady," the others replied, "With all my heart." This old custom was observed every day. At Christmas another old custom was observed. Hot spiced ale and toast was ready by six o'clock in the morning for anyone who chose to come to the Castle for it. They used to drink it out of soup plates with spoons, soaking the toast in the beer. We used to make a laundry clothes basket full of toast. His Lordship used to call Christmas day "Red face day," for when we were all assembled in the little church, which was just across the moat, he could see us all, with faces like peoneys. I used to sing in the choir, and on Christmas morning everyone did "let out" when singing the well known hymns—they had to: the hot toast and ale made them do it.

A silver tankard of the same stuff was handed round in the dining room every Christmas at dinner. When the mummers came, they went away full up and quite merry. His Lordship used to tell the story that on going for a walk one Christmas morning, after the village band had been to the Castle to play, on going across the park he came across one fellow lying in the snow hugging a big brass bass, a little farther on another with a trombone, another farther on with a cornet, and the fellow with the big drum could not get over the stile at all. They were not used to having home brewed ale. They were all lying scattered about in the snow. I never knew his Lordship speak to an under servant. He spoke to me once when I was trying to ride an old-fashioned fifty-two inch bicycle in the stable yard. He was walking through: he said: "Funny horse to ride, isn't it?" He was never known to speak in the House of Lords, but once, then he said to an attendent: "Will you please shut that window." Servants seldom wanted to leave that place, unless they had been there some time and wanted promotion. I think what kept them together to a great extent was we were allowed a dance on the first Tuesday in every month. The mason, who worked on the estate, played the 'cello, his son played second fiddle, the tailor played first violin. I played sometimes as well. The tailor's father had played at the Castle before him; in fact it had been an acknowledged institution as long as anyone could remember. The under gardeners, the grooms, the two whips from the kennels, and perhaps a friend or two would come in, so there was no lack of partners for the maids. Sometimes when visitors were staying in the Castle the ladiesmaids and valets would come in the servants' hall. The tables were put on one side, which formed a band stand. Our programme consisted of lancers, quadrilles, waltzes, schottisches, polkas, Valse of Vienna, Polka Mazurka, and country dances. Fox-trots, jazz, bunnyhugs, and shimmy shakes, all those sort of dances had not been dreamt of in those days. Everything was conducted in a decent style, no rowdyism. Sometimes someone would sing a song between the dances. The young servants soon learnt to dance, and could dance the lancers with the best of them. I would play my violin after supper for them to practice when opportunity offered. I think this sort of thing keeps servants together, makes them just one great big happy family. Sometimes the younger sons of the Earl, when home from College, would come in, but not before knocking the door and asking if they may. There were several sons and daughters of the Earl still unmarried. In the winter, during the College vacations, they would get a licence from the Lord Chamberlain and play theatricals, in aid of her Ladyship's hospital. Of course, I was in it. In one part I played the part of a woman. A dresser came from London, and rouged and painted our faces, also provided the costumes and wigs, also scenery. These plays lasted a week. The Curate was prompter. We rehersed in a large room in the Castle: it was very interesting fun. One of my faults in playing, of which, no doubt, I had many, was that I always "played to gallery." I knew I should get very little applause from the gentry, they knowing I was a servant: their exertions in that direction being the exertion of tapping their thumb nails together, and perhaps not that, but when I saw a chance of a "gag," I put it in.

To illustrate this I will set down what happened when I sang at a concert some years later; in one of the Eastern Counties. The lady got up the affair in aid of one of her charities. I was butler there. The house was full of company for the occasion, most of the performers were of the family, or visitors staying in the house. I was the only "commoner," the others being all gentry. After an early dinner we all drove to the Town Hall. Previously I had practiced my songs in the front hall, one of the young ladies playing the piano. No remarks were made about the songs, except that one of the gents said, "That fellow can sing," but they had never seen me in "character." I slipped a hat box under the seat when starting, and I knew a little about "making up." It was a crowded house. The concert began by one of the ladies showing them how well she could play the piano. Then one or two songs or duets, about the moon and love mixed. When it drew near my turn I began to "make up." Of course I was simply ignored by the gentry behind the scenes. I thought to myself, after all that milk and water I will give you something stronger. I had a pair of large check trowsers, a white top hat with black band, a good false moustashe, black coat with buttonhole, white spats, and a cane, not forgetting the rouge. I sang my best. I never sang a song on a stage better; it was serio-comic,

and I fancy rubbed the gentry up the wrong way
in parts. With a few dance steps, and a trick
or two I simply "brought down the house." I
seldom suffered from stage fright, the remedy for
which is to keep moving about. Well, nothing but
an "encore" would please them; so I gave them a
lively solo on my violin, which did the trick again.
The gallery wanted more, but the gentry would
not let me go on again. Then came the interval.
I noticed the rest of the performers go into a
corner, and hold a conference. Then one of the
gents came over to me and said, "We have decided
that you shall not go on in the second part of the
concert. Miss Soandso will sing in your place."
I nearly said "Damn," but I didn't. When my
turn came round, and the lady began to sing, the
whole back of the hall shouted, "Where's Horne?
We want Horne; bring him out." They would
not let her sing for some minutes. When they
found it was no good she went on with her song.
In any case I would not have gone on again:
"See them hanged first." There's gentry; jealous because I got better encores than they did.

But let us get back to the moated Castle.
These plays went off very well, and were a finan-
cial success, as no one but the dresser from London
went to the treasury for wages. One night,
though I was "word perfect," I was on the stage
talking my part to a man sitting on the opposite

side of a table, when everything became a blank. I had lost my cue; my back being towards the promter I could not catch it for a bit. I had let my mind wander. But, altogether, those were jolly times.

One curious thing happened one summer evening. I had got a large tray loaded with dishes of desert from the stillroom: on one of the dishes was a round green melon, one of those with network all over them. To get to the dining room I had to open a green baize door, which would only open by pulling it towards me. I rested the tray on one knee, opening the door; on doing so the melon rolled off the tray, and being downhill, it went off down the passage "on its own." All right, thinks I, I will come back for you directly. On going back no melon was to be seen. I asked the stillroom maid if she had seen it; she said no. No one else was about at the time. I looked everywhere, then I went out on the drawbridge. There I saw the melon bobbing about in the moat. I rushed to the front door, got the punt, poled round, and captured it. The stones in the passage had become worn through the years of use, that a channel had been made in the centre; just the place for a round melon to go carreering in, the farther it went, the faster it went, in its wild and giddy flight. As I always had three or four hours to myself every afternoon, which I devoted to studying photography, music, and the violin, for I could always lay the dinner cloth directly the footmen had cleared away the lunch, as none of the gentry went into the dining room except to meals. I found that the old ale was a detriment to study; so determined to give it up, as after a good dinner, and plenty of ale, I always felt inclined for a nap. It was a strain at first, but after the first month it was easy to go without it. I have kept it up for the last thirty years, and my intelect is clearer without it. Though by doing it I lost many friends. Even now I have no objection to going into a public-house with friends. They have what they like, I have ginger ale. But they soon get tired of that, and say: "Oh, he's no good; he's a blooming 'Tote.'" But it is a curious thing that when servants meet the first question is, "Going to have a tonic?"

I got to know the aforesaid photographer, he was a nice fellow. He said if I came to his place he would soon put me in the way of it, and in three months would be able to take a decent photo. I should also be a help to him. So I used to bike over to the little town every afternoon and get to work. He taught me retouching, and how to shade off a photo. He said: yours is a very precarious profession; for the least fault, real or imaginary, out you go, with a reference that will be of little or no use to you. Now, I will put something in your hands that they cannot take away. In the end I invested in a ten pound camera, and have made it pay for itself over and over again.

It took me two years to get all the silver in good order, there was such a lot of it. When I first went there the silver plates and dishes were firstly taken to the stillroom to be washed, and then brought to the pantry to be washed again. They carried them in laundry clothes baskets, but that was knocking it about too much for me, so I stopped it, and they were taken straight from the dining room to the pantry. The stud groom, under gardener, and grooms came in and "washed up," so that by the time I came out of the dining room silver and glass was all washed and put away; there was no lack of help. One piece of solid silver, a wine cooler, took four men to carry it to the dining room, there was also immense quantities of ornamental antique silver. I would never work so hard at silver again, to get it to perfection for others to benefit by it. Blistered hands were quite a common thing.

CHAPTER VI

WE had an annual cricket match and sports in the park, between servants of another large house not far off and our own servants. On one occasion we were practising racing, when the Earl passed. He said, in fun, "There they go, running for a gallon of my beer." On one occasion when playing in a cricket match the opposing batsman sent up a "skyer." I had to step backwards, keeping my eye on the ball, to make a catch; the ball came down on the top of my thumb, knocking the top joint down level with the lower joint. My little dumpty thumb did look comical, but I did not let it set, but pulled it quickly back into its place again, but my hand went black with the bruise. The sports ended up with a good supper, plenty of tobacco, and long churchwarden clay pipes, which are seldom seen now-a-days, songs, and a speech or two, all tending to good fellowship. Of course our "String Band" came, and the maids, and all who wished danced on the cricket ground before the supper. The injury to my thumb reminds me of an incident that happened. Often when visiting valets are staying in a house, they will help the butler wait dinner, if there is a large party. On

this occasion a valet was waiting dinner; the gentleman noticed that his servant's thumb nail was
black and looked dirty.   The next time his valet
handed him something he slipped a piece of paper
into the valet's hands: on it was written, "Go and
clean your nails."   The valet wrote underneath,
"Please, Sir, it's where I hit it with a hammer,"
and slipped it into his Master's hand when handing him the next dish.   Though this having to
wait dinner is not liked by visiting valets.

There was a place near Ashby de la Zouche
where the butler had no difficulty in that matter.
(For it is no joke to wait dinner after a day's
shooting and loading, also having to clean the guns,
and shooting clothes, and perhaps dry them ready
for the next day.)   At this place (I won't mention
names) the butler kept a list of the valets who had
helped him wait dinner.   When your visit ended
a brace of phesants and a hare, or a brace of phesants and two rabbits, with a label with the valet's
name on was given him to take back to London.

One does not generally get as much as "Thank
you" for waiting dinner when visiting, though by
doing so you save them employing and paying
waiters.   The usual trick is for the valets to hop
off out of the way to the village or town, to avoid
being asked to wait, or to say they have not
brought their dress clothes with them.

At the above-mentioned place the dress liveries

of the footmen were most striking. They wore
white coats, black breeches and waistcoats, black
silk stockings, silver buckles, powdered hair; the
liveries were profuse in silver lace, but the peculiar
part was they wore a kind of loose velvet outside
sleeve which had a tassel at the end: a memorium
of an ancestor, who in a scrap or battle of some
sort (the enemy having caught him by the sleeve)
tugged till the sleeve came out, leaving it in the
enemy's hand, and he so escaped.

It must be forty-five years ago when the following incident happened. At the time I was third
footman to the Earl of ——. The house was full
of company, with a lot of visiting valets staying
at the Castle. After our work was finished for
the night, about a dozen or so footmen and valets
used to congregate in the pantry to play "nap."
The butler did not object as long as we did not
make a noise. Sometimes they played till well on
into the morning. The under butler and second
footman slept in the pantry in let down beds.
One night the second footman (a six foot young
fellow) did not want to play any longer, but
wanted to go to bed, but could not do so, as the
card players were in the way, he could not let down
his bed. He kept worrying them about it, saying, "I want to go to bed, you fellows; I got to be
up early." "Oh, shut up, you silly fool," but he
would not shut up, so they bundled him into the

plate room; a kind of vault with an iron air-tight door to keep the valuable plate from tarnishing, but they forgot about it being air-tight. He went to sleep in a different way. When they had finished playing cards they unlocked the iron door to let him out. There he lay on the stone floor, apparently dead. We carried him out, and by putting the ammonia bottle under his nose, and rubbing him, he gradually came round and opened his eyes.

Just a word about the hair powdering business. I have often thought how much better it would have been for each footman to have had a wig made of white hair, tied at the back with a black ribbon bow, each man to have his block to put it on when not in use, the footman to keep his hair cut very short, so that it did not show. It would be much better than the powder, for when I did it I constantly had a cold in the head through having to re-powder after going out with the carriage, one's head is seldom dry. But I am tumbling over myself. Let us get back to the moated Castle again.

I always got back from my music or photo lesson at seven o'clock, in time to get the silver plates hot for dinner, make the salad and mayonaise sauce, and get into my dress livery, in fact everything ready by eight o'clock. I also kept my eyes open, and learnt all there was to learn for my next step up the ladder; namely, to be a valet.

It is no uncommon thing when entertaining Royalty for the entertainers to borrow servants from their friends for the occasion, in the same way the poor borrow a frying pan, flat iron, or a rub of the soap, thus showing a servant is considered as a chattel, "Do what you like with them" sort of idea.

A curious antique "toast" servants had amongst themselves, a sort of jangle, ran thus:—

"Here's to those that are in, here's to those that are out,
May the Devil turn him inside out
That tries to get his fellow servant out."

The idea is there, but the poetry is rotten.

Betting is the downfall of a great many servants. Probably more so now than ever it was. The mid-day papers show plainly what is going on, and give tips. It all looks so simple, and an easy way to get money for nothing. I have nothing to say against betting or any other game, the only harm is when one invests more than one can afford to lose. The servant generally has a few shillings to spare: he has not to pay for his clothes, lodgings, or food, and generally has his humble shilling or two on, when he had far better have bought himself a couple of pairs of socks. I have

dabbled in it in a small way. (The poor must
have a little spice in their lives, for their lives are
drab enough.) Though taking it altogether, I am
sure I am out of pocket. The game is far too
intricate for ordinary mortals. The game con-
sists of the following emotions, hope, doubt, disappointment, remorse. Still, they go at it again the
next day, hoping to retrieve their losses, and a bit
more: they go through the same emotions again,
and so the game goes on.

I mentioned previously about the butler at this
place coming a "cropper." He used to bet far
more than he could afford: a disreputable fellow
used to come from the town every morning to take
his commissions.

It is an old saying, "Give him enough rope,
and he will hang himself." Well, he did it.
About six months after I left he got the "Order
of the Boot." He managed to get a situation with
another Noble Earl. Still he could not leave the
gee-gees alone.

On the family coming to London for the season,
certain drawing room ornaments, such as antique
watches, brooches, medals, jewels, bric-a-brac, that
was all kept in a plate chest of its own. These
things were not displayed as they should have been.
Her Ladyship told him to put them out; still they
did not appear; he said he could not find the key.
At last they lost all patience. His Lordship

came down to the pantry.   The butler said he had
not found the key.   His Lordship sent for a carpenter and burst the chest open.   It was empty.
The next thing his Lordship did was to send to
Vine Street Police Station.   Shortly afterwards
two gentlemen in plain clothes appeared.   Then
the butler made a clean breast of it, showed them
no end of pawn tickets, and collapsed generally.
At the trial he was found guilty and sentenced to
six months.

The last I heard of him was that he was seen
outside a pub in the north of London, holding
horses' heads.   So that's that.

No: betting is best left alone altogether, unless
one has the will power, and knows how far to go,
and when to stop.   It is an exciteing but fatal
pastime.

The time soon came round for us to pack up, to
go to Scotland to pay our attentions to the grouse
and salmon.

During all this time my youngest sister and her
"waster" of a husband had found their way to our
home.   He would not work at a job for any length
of time, and by his disgraceful "goings on," and
staying out at all hours of the night, he was gradually driving my mother into her grave, as eventually he did his wife.   Such was the state of affairs when my brother, not being able to find any
suitable work round that part of the country, was

obliged to return to gentleman's service, leaving
my mother in the care of my youngest sister. He
happened to get a place as footman at a house
in Scotland, about four miles from us, but seperated by the river Tay. We both had bicycles,
and used to meet each other, perhaps half-way.
On one of these occasions I was a little late in
starting, so thought I would take a short cut that
would save me a mile and a half if I went by the
road. I had previously walked down this path
to the ferry, and took my chance of riding down it
on my fifty-two inch old-fashioned bike. These
bikes had a happy knack of pitching one over the
front wheel at the least provocation, such as meeting a stone in the road, and invariably the small
wheel at the back would come over and hit one on
the back of the neck. Often on going downhill
the brake would not have sufficient power. To
save myself I have often ran the bike straight into
a hedge at the side of the road. The consequence
was the bike was left on one side of the hedge, and
I was on the other side in the field. They were
dangerous things to ride. One advantage was one
could see the country, perched up so high.

Well, I turned the bike into the path that led
down to the ferry, the path winded in and out
among the rocks: the farther I got the faster I
went. It required a lot of dexterity to steer between them. Eventually my front wheel hit a

rock full butt.   I went over the front handles like
a stone out of a catapult.   Instead of hedges at
the sides of the roads in Scotland there are mostly
rough stone walls; one of these stopped me from
going any farther.   When I woke up I found I
sat in a deep narrow ditch.   I was looking at my
toes, blood was running from a wound in my head
and side of my face, all down the front of my coat.
The stocking and breeches were clean cut off one
knee, also all the flesh off my knee cap.   I pulled
myself together, got my bike, which had gone on
a bit down the hill and toppled over.   I went back
to the house, and asked them how long I had been
gone; they said half an hour, so that I had been
in the land of Nod about twenty minutes.   So I
did not see my brother that day.   One does not
like turning back, but sometimes it is wise.   For
my part I always like to go forward, and take the
consequences.   Lot's wife was turned into a piller
of salt for looking back: but a fellow told me the
other day his wife looked back and turned into a
pub.   One cannot retrieve the past, but it is wise
to avoid past mistakes, and do better in the future.

At the place in Scotland there was one man in
addition, a baker, thus making eight men in the
house.   The baker, besides making the bread,
when visitors were in the house, had to put on dress
livery, like the footmen, and appear at the front.
About thirty servants sat down to dinner in the

servants' hall—the steward's room party never
came in—but all livery stablemen came in, and
they were not a few, including two postilions.   A
long boat, mounted on wheels, was used for taking
out the shooting parties, drawn by four grey
horses.   The postilions had a large silver badge on
their left arms, which bore the crest of the family.
The stern of the boat was furnished most luxur-
iously with silk cushions for the gentry, the servants and guns rode in the bows of the boat.   I
never saw the boat taken off the wheels.   It was
twenty feet long, and was intended for crossing
rivers where there were no bridges.

On occasions when the family go to Scotland in
August the Butler has to superintend the convey-
ance of all luggage by rail, from one house to another, and see that nothing is lost.   I myself have
had over a hundred packages to take to Scotland
by passenger train.   I may have been fortunate,
but I have never lost anything at any time.   The
best way is to arrange with the railway company
to convey it as "Luggage in bulk."   On one of
these occasions a curious thing happened.   Travelling by the same train was a certain Duchess
going on a visit to another Duchess farther North
than our place, and the station we got out at.   We
had several gentlemen and lady visitors going to
our place by the same train.   On arrival at our
station all our luggage was put out on the plat-

form, then carted up to the house, and taken to the different rooms they were to occupy. All the gun and cartridge cases, fishing rods, etc., taken to the gun room. It takes a bit of management to get everyone settled, including servants in a large house. Finally we all got settled down and in working order. In the next day's papers we read that a certain Duchess had lost her jewel case when travelling to the North of Scotland on the previous day. They were supposed to be stolen "en route," and were valued at ten thousand pounds. After a fortnight shooting our first batch of visitors left to make room for another batch. On looking round as usual to see that the valets, loaders, or ladiesmaids had taken all their belongings with them, I saw in the gun room what appeared to be a cartridge case in the corner, which certainly did not belong to any of our family. On examination I saw it had a railway label for a station farther North but no address label. I thought it best to send it to our stationmaster, as no doubt he may have had enquiries about it, since none of our house party just gone had owned it. So, as a gillie was going to the station with a small cart, I gave him the case, telling him to give it to the stationmaster. About two months after this some of the factor's boys were playing about outside, making no end of a noise, that I went out and told them to be quiet. They shouted to me,

"Mr Butler, come and see what we have found."
I, thinking it was a "catch," said, "Run away,
with your noise." But one said, "Do come, it's
a box." I went, and saw in the small luggage
cart the very case I had given the gillie to take to
the stationmaster two months before. I sent for
him. He said he had put the case in the cart when
I gave it to him, but having occasion to use a larger
cart, he pushed the small cart to the back of the
shed, and forgot all about it. The cart was partly
covered with hay which was stored there, it was
seldom used and might have staid there all the
winter, being too small for conveying much luggage. The case was at once taken to the stationmaster, and proved to be the Duchess' jewel case,
containing the ten thousand pounds' worth of
jewellery, and for which detectives had hunted
over the whole country, and further, to find. We
quickly had a visit from a detective, who wormed
out the facts of the affair. I got a wigging from
the Bos for not being smarter about things, and
was told to hold myself in readiness to go before
the magistrates. However, the Bos wrote and
explained to the Duchess, the Duchess replied that
she always packed her jewell case inside a strong
rough-looking leather case, in the guard's van, as
they travelled safer that way. As I did not hear
anything more about it I suppose it ended up sat-

isfactorily. The jewel case had been put out of
the train with our luggage by mistake.

Another remarkable affair was the six pipers.
Immediately the cloth was removed from the dining room table the large doors at the end of the
room were thrown open; three of them went one
side of the table, three the other: they crossed at
the bottom, playing all the time; then marched
out of the room. This has been done in several
large houses I have visited in Scotland. Also a
piper would play in the corridor outside the Earl's
bedroom, when he was called every morning at
eight o'clock, though at some places they march
round the outside of the Castle at that time in the
morning. The pipes sound nice at a distance, but
inside a house, at close range, I think it rotten, the
notes have not space enough to disentangle themselves from each other. I suppose one has to be
cultured up to a taste for it.

A curious custom in Scotland was that every
servant had the care of their own knife, fork and
spoon. You took them to meals with you and
took them away again. I don't know why; some
put them on a ledge underneath the table opposite
their seat.

On shooting mornings the house steward would
lock himself in his wine cellar, and open a little
hatch, like a ticket office at a railway station. The

valets and loaders would queue up, hand in his and his Master's flask, when they were handed back filled with whiskey: this took place every morning at a certain time, and woe betide you if you were late.

An incident occurred one season when in Scotland. A footman was clearing away breakfast, when he set to work carving a few thick slices off one of the hams in the breakfast room, he thinking there was no one about. I don't know why he did it, except it was from sheer greed, as we always got plenty of good food in the servants' hall. His Lordship, who stood in the deep recess of one of the windows coughed, he had seen it all. The footman dropped the carving knife and fork, put the slices of ham in a napkin, and bundled it into the sideboard drawer. Then his Lordship appeared and said: "Send the house steward to me!" He came. His Lordship said, "Send that footman back to London by the next train." He went.

A similar incident happened in a large house, the home of a Noble old Marquis. The dinner in the dining room was finished. The butler with his friend, the groom of the chambers, went to the dining room to take away his wines, and to ring the bell twice for the footmen to come and clear the room. Taking the port decanter, he poured out two glasses full: giving one to the groom of the chambers, he said: "Well, here's the Noble Lord's health; may the old duffer live till he's a hundred," when a small voice from the recesses of a deep armchair in front of the fire said: "Thank you for your sentiments, but I don't thank you for drinking my port wine." The butler thought everyone had left the room.

I often got a chance of my favourite sport, tickling up the rabbits. I borrowed a gun from the head keeper. One day I put up a woodcock, and could not resist, so brought it down. This was the only woodcock I ever shot. I also only caught one salmon "on my own." He lent me an old salmon rod. I used to get up as soon as it was light in the morning, and off down to the banks of the river Tay. The salmon flies I whipped off, or hung up in the trees or bushes were legion: casting is a fine art, and takes time to do it properly.

One morning at the very first cast I "got him." I played him for half an hour. I did not have a gaf with me. How to land him? that was the question. When I got him near the bank he caught sight of me. Away he went again. I was afraid he would go over a waterfall a short distance down the river, and snap the line. It is very exciting to feel the electric quiver come up the line.

I laid the rod on the bank, keeping hold of the

line; ran my hands up to the top of the rod, still holding the line, walked up to my waist in the water, and gradually drew the salmon near and nearer towards me. Eventually I caught him by the tail, and took him to the bank. When I left go one hand he sprung away and was off down the bank into the water again, but he did not get far. I had seen the keepers strike them between the eyes with a stone or a short club, and so kill it instantly. I tried it: the salmon bounded up three or four feet in the air, and was nearly in the water again. I got him back, and repeated the dose.

Just then I heard a roar of laughter from the rocks above me: it was a keeper who had been watching my antics. He came down and killed the salmon. It was an eighteen pounder, and clean run. Although I was not actually poaching, in the strict sense of the word, I was enjoying a bit of sport reserved for the rich, and "much too good for poor people."

I have often been trolling with the keepers in a boat, with three rods out at the stern of the boat, which is rowed backwards and forwards across the river, it being allowed to float down a few yards each time the boat crosses. Suddenly one of the reels start spinning, and the line runs out at a great rate. We have hooked a fish. While one man plays the fish, another reels in the two vacant lines, the boat is rowed ashore. The fish is played from the bank, a man stands with a gaf ready in the boat, the fish is brought up alongside the boat, and gaffed. Sometimes eight or a dozen salmon can be caught in this way in one day's sport. And good sport it is. We used to take enough lunch for all, not forgetting a dram or two. Many were the tales we told, and jokes we cracked, while sitting in the boat, waiting for the reels to start whizing round, and make their welcome noise. I can remember a few of them; but for an Englishman to talk broad Scotch it is a good plan to put three or four hazel nuts or pebbles in one's mouth before one can get the "crack" of it. I will relate one or two of them:—A Scotch man and woman were having a few words. She said: "Mon, if I had a husband like you, I'd gie him pizen." The man replied: "If I had a wife like you, by Gad, I'd take it."

But for a dry and mouldy one the following one takes the oatcake:—A man was sitting in a tramcar reading a paper, when a man o'er fu' o' whiskey got in and sidled up to the man reading the paper, and said:—"Mon, did ye see me get on the car?" "Aye, I saw ye." After a while the o'er fu' man said, "D'ye ken me?" "Na, I dinna ken ye, and dinna want." "Then how d'ye ken it was me that got on the car?" It took a minute or two before I could see the "gist" of the foregoing, but it is just what a drunken man would say.   I was not to be beaten, so chimed in with the following.

A man, smoking his pipe, was passing the railings of a lunatic asylum.   One of the "patients" said, "I say, mister, that's nice tobacco you are smoking.   Will you give me a pipefull?"   "Oh, yes; you are welcome to a pipefull."   Then the lunatic said: "They put me in this place, but there is nothing wrong with me.   But they will never let me out again, and as you are so kind I will tell you where I hid all my money, at the foot of a certain tree before they caught me, if you will bring me a pound of this tobacco, at this time to-morrow."   The man thought it a good chance to get rich quick, so he said he would.   On the morrow, he brought the pound of tobacco, and handed it to the lunatic, and said, "Now, tell me where you hid the money."   The "lunatic" replied: "Come inside."

Then another said:—"I was looking down the advertisements in the paper the other day, when I saw this: 'A young widow wants washing.'"   He said, "I would have taken the job on myself, but I was in a hurry, and had to catch a train."

Another said:—"A Jew and his son were waiting for a 'bus.   When the 'bus did arrive, and they were about to get on a man rushed up and pushed them aside, so that they were left behind.   The following remarks were made: "That was a very

rude man, fadder, to push us away from the 'bus."
"Yes, my son, he was a very rude man." "Fadder, don't you think he ought to be punished?
Will God punish him?" "He is allready punished, my son, for I have got his watch."

Yet another:—"Two peppery gents were walking down Piccadilly in opposite directions and met
full butt. Both said, 'Beg pardon,' and side
tracked, but both side-tracked the same way:
'Beg pardon,' again. One of them was cross-
eyed. After another re-shuffle, one trod on the
other's favourite corn. "I wish you would look
where you are going," said the cross-eyed one.
"Sorry," said the other, "but I wish you would
go where you are looking."

Then there was a sudden whizzing of one of the
reels. We had caught another fish, which put an
end to our tale telling. There is many a day's
sport not half so enjoyable as a day's trawling,
perhaps catching a dozen salmon, perhaps none at
all. But to illustrate the saying that a "little"
knowledge is dangerous, I will relate what happened to my brother and I on a salmon fishing
stunt. We had arranged to meet just below a
certain waterfall above Perth. I got permission
to take one of the boats from the keeper, he knowing we could both row. My brother was to row,
while I cast with the salmon rod, he to keep the
boat just out of the rough water of the river (which

was just after a spate), and letting the boat down
the river gradually. I had a few casts, when I
found he had let the boat get into the rough water.
At that instant, the boat going down the river at
a terrific rate, the bottom of the boat struck an
under-water rock. I went overboard into the
rough water. Luckily, I caught the gunwale of
the boat with two fingers, the force of the water
held my body floating out straight. The boat—
being flat-bottomed—stuck on the rock. We
stared at each other for a second or two. I saw
the rod was broken. I forced my legs down till I
felt the rock with my feet, told my brother to put
the two other oars ready in the rowlocks. We had
to be quick, as the water was dashing over the
bows of the boat. I wobbled the boat till I found
it moving, sprang in, grasped the oars, and pulled
with all our might out of the rough water. As it
was we were carried down the river a good distance
but got into the back-water just in time to prevent
the boat being smashed against some rocks. Then
we rested a bit to get our breath. We went that
distance in a few minutes, but it took us two hours
to get the boat back to the place we found it.
These boats are sometimes landed, and taken up
the river in carts, especially if there is a bend in
the river, which is much easier than rowing them
up against the stream. This was, I think, the last
of my attempts at salmon fishing on my own ac-

count, and the third near squeak from my being drowned. The Scotch are well known to be a thrifty people, as the following tale will show:—
"An old Scotch gentleman died. In the conditions of his will, in order to get their share of his money, his three sons had to say a short prayer, and put a sovereign in his coffin to be buried with him. The two youngest did this. Then the elder brother came, said his prayer, took out the two sovereigns, and put in a cheque for three pounds."

In this place they kept up the old custom of family prayers. At nine o'clock every morning the bell on the tower would ring, and servants assembling from all directions, the maids tying on clean aprons, the men putting on their livery coats, all queuing up, and marching in when all were ready, the maids on one side, the men on the other, of the Baronial Hall.

There is a story of a young housemaid who did not appear at prayers. The housekeeper asked her the reason why. She replied that she did not like his Lordship always praying "at" her. When his Lordship read out, "O, Lord, who hatest nothing thow hast made," she thought he said, "O Lord, who hatest nothing but the housemaid."

Well, taking it altogether, I don't think these prayers did the servants a bit of good: for no matter what job they had in hand at the time, they had to leave it, and rush to prayers.

In Ireland, at a large place we were once on a
visit, half the servants were Roman Catholic.   At
a given time each morning they would down tools,
and rush off to the town to Mass.   The others left
behind being Protestant had to finish their jobs.

It seems a curious religion that, no matter
what sin, backbiting, lying or slandering, or even
worse, by going to Confession, everything is
wiped off the slate, so to speak, and they are free
to begin the game all over again.   But what
I cannot make out is, what happens to the one that
has been sinned against, the damaged one, where
does he, or she, come in, if no reparation is made
bodily and spiritually?   Perhaps I do not know
enough about it.   But I never would believe that
there is any man on this earth who ever wore
trowsers, or kilts for that matter, who has any
power whatever to forgive sin.   It simply can't be
done.   Arguing about religion is a fruitless game,
and always ends up at the point you began at.
We will conclude that all roads lead to Heaven,
providing it is the narrow one.   The broad and
easy road leads to destruction, both of mind and
body in the end.

CHAPTER VII

AFTER going through the daily routine with this Noble family for several years as under butler I thought I would blossom out into a full-blown valet. As I could clean and load a gun, clean a scarlet coat, top boots and leather breeches with the best of them: also I knew enough about fishing, and what to do on a salmon fishing expedition. Drying the lines, and clothes, etc., ready for the next morning, and dry all the flies that had been used. I felt I wanted to see a bit more of the world before I settled down to the humdrum life of a butler. So I sent in my notice to leave, and soon got a place as valet to a single young gentleman. Now a valet, as a rule, thinks "no small beer of himself." He aims to dress as smart as his master, and puts plenty of oil on his hair, and generally wears a finger ring. And more credit to him for being smart, for he has to turn out his Master's clothes and boots to perfection, as well as his own. But the valet, like the butler, pure and simple, will soon be as extinct as the Dodo: his duties being merged into those of a footman or groom of the chambers, and soon parlourmaids will be doing the whole box of tricks. The young gentleman I valeted was a nice, sensible man, but being the younger son of an Earl, was not overweighted by this world's goods. He was tall and slim, and rode well to hounds, and was a good shot. He looked well in any sort of clothes, but especially his hunting kit. He was well sought after for country house parties, especially by the ladies. He played the violin nicely, and could sing a song. He had a suite of rooms, now called a flat, and when the London season was over he got no end of invitations. It was pack up and off we would go, not forgetting to take his violin, and my own as well, for he knew I could play. I always took my camera as well. On one occasion we visited the house of a certain Earl in the Midlands. The occasion was to celebrate the birth of a son and heir. It was to be a lively week. A gentrys' ball, a farmers' ball, and a servants' ball, besides all kinds of sports in the park. There was a brass band playing to dancing in the park, and a string band at night. There were thirty gentry in the house, the steward's room was full, also the servants' hall. In those days one would not think of going into the steward's room to supper unless dressed in a black bob-tailed coat, white shirt and black bow tie. In fact, one would be told of it, if he did not, even if he had been out shooting all day. In the servants' hall they

were not so particular.   There were about a dozen
visiting valets, and a corresponding number of
ladies' maids.   We were all expected to lend a
hand on ball nights, which we did willingly.   On
the night of the farmers' ball my room mate (a
visiting valet who slept in the same room as myself
over the stables, for the mansion was full up) were
alloted to take charge of the cloak room, which
was a sort of counter rigged up in the front hall.
It was amusing when the farmers and tradesmen
and their ladies departed they would ask when we
handed them their hats and coats, "What's to pay?"
"Oh, no charge," we replied; but they would leave
something.   Some twopence, others sixpence, and
so on.   We found we got so much ready cash that
we put one of the farmer's old top hats on the floor,
and tossed the money into it.   When it was all
over we emptied the money out into a handkerchief
and took it to our bedroom to divide.   We found
we had sixteen and eightpence each, mostly cop-
pers.   On the other ball nights we waited at the
buffet, and at the supper.   On the day the park
was thrown open to all-comers a dinner was given
to about five hundred; each man as he entered was
given three tickets, entitling him to three pints of
old ale.   Some of the old fellows were not used
to such strong stuff.   When they came out from
the riding school (where the dinner was served, all
decorated with flags and mottos, the pillars were

entwined with different colours) some of them went on their backs, with heels up in the air.

Tea tents were all over the place, and farm waggons for biting flour, and treacle bags, and apples, with the competitors' hands tied behind their backs, causing no end of fun. Wheel-barrow loads of cooked potatoes were wheeled to the riding school, wrapped in table cloths, and the rate at which the food disappeared was alarming. At night there was a grand display of fireworks.

In the afternoon I got busy with my camera, a half plate. First I had to take the house party at the front door. That done, I had to take the crowd. This I could not do on the ground, as everybody wanted to be in front, and got close up to the camera. So I commandeered one of the farm waggons. There were plenty of willing hands to pull it to the spot I wanted. It turned out to be a good picture, with the mansion in the background. I worked a few clowds in the sky. I quickly got orders for a hundred copies, which I finished on our return to London, and mounted them on good cards, at one shilling each, which paid me well. The gentry were mightily pleased with their group. A thousand gallon tun of ale was brewed to be broached when the heir attained the age of twenty-one. Alas, the baby when he grew up was killed in the Great War. As on the nights between the balls there was not so much to do, they had arranged to have a dance in the steward's room, inviting a few friends to come in. We hurried over supper, and had got the tables cleared away, when a footman came and told me my "Bos" wanted to see me in the front hall. He said they had got the ball room partly lit up, and asked if I would play my violin for the house party to dance. I said I had lent my violin (which was true, but only for a short time, as a fellow was then trying to get a tune out of it), I thinking I should thus get out of it. "Well," he said, "you can go up to my room and get my violin." It was a beautiful instrument. So I was fairly in for it. So I went in and mounted the dias where the band played on ball nights. They asked me to play a valse. I soon warmed to my work, and let go for all I was worth: and kept them going from nine-thirty till twelve-thirty with lancers, valses, polkas, quadrilles, but it was mostly valses they wanted. It is the only time I ever made bishops, priests, and I was going to say, kings,—there was a Prince there—hop it. Well, I thought I should not get less than a sovereign for this night's work. When they had finished they all walked round and thanked me, and said, "You play very nicely." But I got "Nothing," and lost the fun in the steward's room as well. But on the morning we came away I was standing at the carriage door when the Noble Earl came out of the front door with my Bos. The Earl had his hands in his pockets rattling something, keys I expect, and I thought to myself, now for my sovereign for playing the violin. No: I got nothing. But they had ordered eight mounted photos of the crowd, to stick in their albums as a momento. These I took to their London house shortly after. They asked, "how much." I said, "A sovereign," which was the price a professional photographer would have charged. So I got my sovereign after all.

I remember that family in the old Lord's time. It was quite different then. He kept a full staff, with only himself in the house. The hall porter used to powder, though he had no hair on his head, except a rim round at the back.

Which reminds me of a tale of an old fellow like him, as regards hair. He had the habit, when he was thinking, or very interested in anything, of scratching his pole. It was at a theatre. A boy who sat behind him said: "Chase him out into the open, Gov'nor, you'll catch him then."

This hall porter had thirteen young children. He was left in charge of the town house when the family were away. He used to mend their clothes and boots when on duty in the front hall. When anyone came to the front door he would push the things into the little drawer that is under the seat of his old-fashioned hall porter's chair. Goodness knows what became of him or his family when he

got the sack, for the new Lord did not keep a
hall porter, or groom of the chambers, either; and
I think one of the footmen had to go as well.
Formerly, when they went to Court or some other
important function they made a grand show, the
footmen with three cornered hats, the coachman
also, with his wig. I photographed these liveries
for the guidance of the tailors, both back and
front views; they were covered with gold lace.
Sometimes one meets with an effeminate young
gentleman, generally a younger son of a good
family, who is the idol of the ladies, a sort of carpet
knight; when waited on at table, and handed, for
instance, a dish of cutlets, he will turn every one
of them over in the dish, and then, after all, take
the first one he got hold of. One felt inclined to
put the dish down on the table, and let him get
on with it; besides, he was keeping others waiting.
Again, if he comes into a room in other people's
houses, he will poke the fire, and if he is a fresh
air fanatic, will open the windows.

.   .   .   .

We were never long in one place, but generally
visiting at large houses, except in the "Season"
when we remained in London. I had always been
very fond of reading. I had read all Sir Walter
Scot's novels, and, in fact, every other that I could
get hold of. One large, old house, not far from
Kettering, I was very fond of visiting. It dated

back before Charles the First's time: there were no
modern improvements; everything was just as it
was hundreds of years ago. When my "Bos"
wanted me he used to blow a blast on his hunting
horn across the courtyard. The stone passages
were all bumpy, and up and down hill. The hot
water for baths had to be carried in cans hundreds
of yards. This sort of place appealed to me.
There was the great banqueting hall, with diamond
paned windows from ceiling (which were all hand-
painted) to the floor. A man used to wheel the
fire logs a yard long in a barrow, and stack them
on end, on the great open fireplace. I used to
imagine I could see the ladies and dandies, in their
laces, frills, powdered wigs, and swords, walking
about, as they did in the old days, when ladies
were ladies, and acted as such. The old oil paint-
ings seemed to step out of their frames, and dance
a minuet, and bow and scrape to each other: there
it all was, nothing changed, nothing altered. I
wonder if life was any better in those days than
it is now in these hurry, scurry, "hell for leather,"
can't go fast enough times. In those days if the
King did not suit the people they simply chopped
off his head to stop him talking. Now the Kings
simply hop it, into the adjoining country and live
happily for ever afterwards.

Whenever we went to visit the same place again
the first thing the servants asked me was: "Got

your fiddle?"   As, after supper, if they were tired, they were not too tired for a dance in the servants' hall. We were visiting a large house in Lancashire when I lost my violin. It was dark, on a winter's evening when we arrived at the station. The luggage cart from the house was there to meet us: several other visitors arrived by the same train. I was collecting my small things to take with me in the cab, when the man said, "All right, leave them. I'll bring them all up to the house." I took what I could, but left him to bring my own violin. When he arrived, my violin was not amongst the luggage, he had dropped it on the road. When the company had gone into dinner I walked back to the station, also asked the police, set the town crier, with his bell, going, but all to no purpose. I never saw my violin again. On mentioning the affair, the big Bug of the place said he could not be responsible for his visitors' luggage. Though his own servant had lost it. But I had another violin, still it was a loss to me.

One visit we made was at a Castle in the North of England, the home of a certain Duke. My Bos, I fancied, was sweet on one of the daughters. I saw him come out of one of the rooms looking rather crestfallen. I fancy he had popped the question and had not clicked.

Things went on like this for about two years. Hunting here, shooting there; also attending race meetings, when he was at last captured by the daughter of a magnate in the North of England; and he caught a Tartar. She had plenty of money, but was a regular spitfire. I could not stand her at any price, so handed in my brief, and left him. I was sorry for him in a way, for he was a reasonable young gent to work for.

I was once valet to a Noble Lord who could not bear a vestige of light in his bedroom. When we were travelling I always took large sheets of black Italian cloth. With these I had to fasten over the windows, fanlight, in fact, any little crack or cranny where the light could get in from outside, with drawing pins, and had to take them down in the morning when I called him.

I soon got another valet's place with a gent I will call Sir Henry Cayenne, for he was as hot as they make them, though a gentleman and good sportsman at bottom. He could not open his mouth without swearing. It is said "No man is a hero to his own valet," because he knows too much of his inner life. He hunted three or four days a week, in leathers and scarlet. He had a large house in Yorkshire, and kept a good establishment, butler, valet, two footmen, and an usher, and boy. I found the previous valet had "hopped it" one morning after Sir Cayenne had gone hunting, for on going up to the dressing room he found some of the leather breeches thrown into the bath,

others under the grate, some of the top boots were
thrown out of the window, others in the bath. He
would always have several pairs of each taken up
to choose from. A scarlet coat was also thrown
out of the window. When he returned from hunting he rang his bell, as usual, but no valet appeared. After a while the butler went up. The
Noble Knight said: "Send my valet," with several flowery words entwined. The butler said he
had not seen him all day, for the valet had left the
boots, breeches, and coat, just as he saw them in
the morning, and "hopped it." There was some
sulphorous langwage flying about just then. He
could never keep a valet more than a month or
two; the one previous to the one that "hopped
it" had been in the Life Guards. Though Sir
Cayenne was a six-foot man, he was thin. The
Lifeguardsman was big, and stout as well. One
day they got to words; the valet gave him as good
as he sent, as he did not intend to stay. One of
Sir Cayenne's accomplishments, as well as the
vulgar tongue, was that he was a fairly good boxer.
Sir Cayenne tried to cross the room to where a
lot of hunting crops hung on the wall, saying he
would give the valet a good horse-whipping. "Oh,
no you don't," said the valet, and closed with him,
forcing him backwards on to the bed, and threw
his weight on, and holding Sir Cayenne there.
When he found he could not get free he said, "All

right, I'll give in.   Bring up your book.   I'll pay
it and you can go."   I had not been there but a
day or two when, one morning I was dressing him
for hunting, he said, "Take a clean hunting kit
to —" (some place I did not know) "for I shall
hunt from there to-morrow morning, and sleep
there to-night."   I asked him which was the best
way to get to this place, as I was a stranger, and
did not as yet know the country.   He replied:
"You dam well find out!"   I got hold of the stud
groom, who had been there a good many years.
He told me, and put me up to some of his ways.
Boxing gloves were all over the place, for Sir
Cayenne could box a bit, and was as quick as light-
ening at it.   Sometimes he would get eminent
boxers to come down, and give boxing and weight-
lifting exhibitions in the front hall, inviting the
farmers and their wives to come and see it.   He
had Jackson, the black boxer there, and would put
the gloves on himself and box a round or two with
him.

One day he was lunching alone.   It was his
habit of reading a book at the same time.   He sent
the servants out of the room, a bell was put on the
table for him to ring when he wanted them.   They
were waiting outside in the serving room, when
the footmen took a set of boxing gloves, and began
sparing about.   Sir Cayenne could hear their feet
scuffling on the floor.   He got up and opened the

door and said: "Just stop that b—— game while
I am having my lunch, will you? Or, look here,
just come inside a minute. I will dam soon knock
the stuffing out of you." Needless to say they declined. He used to call the footmen "Brass but-
toned B——s."

There used to be a Royal Duke who could also
use flowery language. One day Sir Cayenne sent
him a palm, saying he was the champion at it.
But the Royal Duke sent it back, saying Sir
Cayenne was the proper claimant, and could not
be beaten, in fact "par excellence." I have heard
that this Royal Duke told his valet that if he was
in his own country, he would shoot him.

I think I can handle a gun as quickly, and load
it as fast as most valets, but to load for Sir
Cayenne was an experience. When the birds began to come over pretty quick he would start
swearing. Not ordinary swearing, but stringing
nothing but swear words together, one after the
other. How he thought of them I can't make out.
If I did not happen to grasp the gun, he would
simply drop it on the ground, which made me late
for the next shot. It is very curious the contrasts
in marriage, for Sir Cayenne had a most beautiful
lady for a wife, as meek and ladylike as he was
blusterous and firey.

At a large luncheon party Sir Cayenne wanted
a second helping of roast beef. The butler being

busy handing the wine one of the footmen carved it off for him. Sir Cayenne shouted out: "Which of you b——s cut this off? You have not given me any b—— fat."

One Sunday afternoon when the butler was out, or asleep, Sir Cayenne rang the library bell. No one answered it. He rang again: still nothing happened. Then he came out into the square stone hall. He could hear a lot of gigling and squealing going on in the servants' hall. The footmen and grooms and second horsemen were in the hall with some of the maidservants. He opened the door and said. "Come out of it. I'll teach you to make a b—— brothel of my house." As they passed out he gave them a bang on the head.

Notwithstanding all his bluster he, like all bullies, was the merest coward in some matters. For instance, he had made up his mind to learn to ride the bicycle. I had to call him an hour earlier every morning to have an hour's practice before breakfast. I had to learn him, and hold him up, but he had no pluck. One day he skidded sideways, and the mud guard scraped all the skin off the shin of my leg. I could feel the blood running down. He said, "Oh, don't show it to me. Don't let me see it. I can't bear the sight of blood." The next morning I went out with a pair of cricketing pads on. He said: "What the

h—— have you got those things on for? We are
not going to play cricket." I said I had quite
enough skin scraped off for the present.

All his carriages were painted black and yellow.
He also drove four-in-hand.

One morning he took his little meek land agent
for a drive to visit some parts of his estate, in a
high two-wheeled cart. He took a short cut across
the park, ran one of the wheels up the bole of a
large tree, and shot them both out. I could not
swear he did this on purpose: but as the Scotch-
man said: "I hae ma doots."

Often I would get twenty minutes' notice to
pack up and be off to London for a night. He
was not stingy with his money: as I used to get five
shillings each way for personal expences. Sir
Cayenne would generally go on to Crewe early to
do some business. I followed by train, and met
him there. He had a leather case with silver fit-
tings, plates and all.   I had to get this packed with
a partridge, or half a cold phesant, and a small
bottle of claret, and get it laid out on the stationmaster's office table, and wait for him. He would
arrive five or ten minutes before the London train
was due.   The train would be ready to start: the
stationmaster told him he could not delay the train
any longer. He would swallow his claret, rush
out, and say to me, "Come on, you silly b——,
you'll lose the train." I would rush out into the

office, grasp the four corners of the table cloth, grab the case, and rush out, to find the station-master holding a door open for me (for he knew Sir Cayenne). Sometimes I would tumble full length on the floor of the carriage, as the train was moving off, and sort the things out afterwards. I dare not be left behind, or I should have got the sack.

After all he was a good sport, and kept up a good house. But the flowery language he used to waste on me was alarming. But I used to keep very cool, and surprising as it may seem, I remained with him over two years. For he paid his valet a hundred a year, and there were other compensations. One day he said to me, "Dam you! Haven't you got any temper at all?" When I first went there all the servants had feather beds. One could flop down and rest. But a new house-keeper that came had them all taken away, and we had to lie on hard mattresses. She was one of these fresh air, hygene fanatics.

The house was surrounded with coal mines, and the miners used to help themselves to Sir Cayenne's game occasionally. One morning we were off to catch the early train for London. He was driving in his high two-wheeled cart, with a groom beside him, and I up behind with the luggage, when a man came through the hedge with a rabbit in his hand. Sir Cayenne threw the reins to the groom, jumped down, took the rabbit away, and beat the man about the head with it, asking him what business he had stealing his game? Interlarded with choice swear words. Then he put his hand into his pocket, threw the man a sovereign, and said, "Damn you, I have no time to stop and talk to you."

Once, shortly after I went into his service, he "let out" and swore at me at a railway station. The air went blue, so sulphroic was his langwage, and in front of a lot of people, and porters too, who did not know him. I thought to myself, "I'll soon put paid to this." So when we got to our destination, and I had him to myself, I told him he could say what he liked to me when we were alone, as it was like water on a duck's back, but if he began it in front of people again I should leave him that minute (unless I was at fault) and he would continue his journey alone. But the greatest display of language occurred when Sir Cayenne was dressing for dinner, and he was trying to tie a white necktie. Sometimes he would spoil twenty before he got one to his satisfaction. I would stand on his left hand and as he spoilt them he threw them down in a heap on the carpet on his right, then I would hand him another. He would not let me tie one for him: but the swear words he strung together was terrific.

When at College he was "Rusticated" for some

of his outrageous escapades; went home, and had a tutor to complete his education. One day he pitched his tutor out of the first floor window, on to the lawn. His study was more like a wild beast show than anything else.

One day we were getting ready for shooting. His dressing room was on the ground floor at the house at which we were visiting. He would always leave everything till the last minute. The other gentlemen were ready and waiting for him outside. One of them was coming towards his window to tell him to hurry, but turned back, and told the others that the air was too blue with language for him to go any closer. Yet, when ladies were about he was the most gentlemanly man of the lot, "Butter would not melt in his mouth."

I put in two years with him, though before I went to him he could not keep a valet for two months. On the day I left him I felt sorry in a way. For although I never crossed him, I could not deny that so much of it played on my nerves. For one is not always such a fool as one looks. I stood in the front hall waiting to be paid off, when he passed and said, "I'll see to you directly." I hardly knew what this meant, so when we went into his room I kept near the fireplace, as I was no match for him at boxing, and was not taking any chances so kept near the poker. On the con-

trary, he was as mild as milk; wrote me out a first-
class reference; gave me a present; shook hands;
he said he was sorry to lose me; and thus we
parted.   I could imagine him living in the time
when duels were in fashion.   He would have had
one on his hands every day of the week.   When
I saw the account of his death some years later, I
felt sorry.   For, though he was such a spitfire,
there was something about him one could not help
liking.   He kept up a good establishment, and a
good house; there was no stint of anything in
reason.   He was not like some of them, always
looking round to find a hook to hang a quarrel
or complaint on.   No, it was just simply "bluster," and his bark was worse than his bite.   He
was a good sport, and he played the game.

CHAPTER VIII

Now I had to scout round and get another place. It was not long before I got hooked on to a Noble Lord—in disposition quite different to my previous Bos, Sir Cayenne. This one turned out to be of a surley disposition. One seldom saw a smile on his face. He was director to several companies, and the employees had cause to keep their eyes open when he was about. Many a man he got sacked, for he was without mercy, a hard-hearted man, and well hated by everyone.

Which reminds me of a little story. At a certain works or factory, two of the men got round a corner to have a few draws of their pipes in working hours. They were busy at it, when they saw a strange man come along. They said: "Come round the corner, mate, or the foreman will see you!" "Well," he replied, "I happen to be the new foreman."

Everybody seemed to hate the sight of this Noble Lord. In the villiage, which belonged to him, the inhabitants never used to touch their hats to him; in fact, never looked at him, or ever had a good word for him. The houses were old and out of repair, the farms also; they could not get

repairs done.   All the dirty work was done by the
estate agent.   One thing he did not forget was
to collect the rents punctually.   The estate agent
was dressed smarter than the Noble Lord, and had
more "Swank."   In fact, one would take him
to be Bos of the show, and as it may be imagined
no one liked him either.   The servants in the
house, or out of it for that matter, did not like
him.   He remarked to the butler one night, "If
this lamp does not burn better there will be a
vacancy for a butler shortly."

The Lord and I used to travel a great deal.
The servants hated the sight of our faces when we
returned home; in fact they treated me like an
unwelcome lodger.   If we happened to arrive
from a long journey between the times for meals,
I could not get anything, but had to wait till the
next meal time came round, though I had missed
my dinner.   The house was fourteen miles from
the railway station.

His Lordship did not go in for fox hunting, but
was keen on shooting and salmon fishing.   His
Lordship's god was his clothes, and himself.   He
had about sixty suits of clothes.   On Sundays he
would make me carry them all downstairs, and
spread them out in a large bedroom on the ground
floor.   When they were all down, I had to go and
tell him they were ready.   When it pleased him
he would come and begin to try them all on, in

front of a long glass, one suit after another, which took hours. When he had finished there was a waggonload of clothes to brush, fold up, and take back to his dressing room, and stack away in their different classes and places. This was the Sunday clothes inspection. But during the two years I was with him he never gave me a thing, not so much as an old worn-out necktie. I have known him catch twenty-eight salmon in a day, ranging from sixteen to thirty-four pounds. But he never gave me one. But they were all packed in boxes and sent by rail to the market, excepting a few to personal friends. Servants were treated by him as though they were a lower order of beings simply sent for his use and convenience.

An amusing incident happened at a shooting party. We were to lunch at a farm house. The late Duke of Cambridge was one of the party. His Highness was very fond of lark pudding. When we arrived at the farm house the gentry went into the parlour, the valets and loaders went into the kitchen, where a table was laid. We put our guns and cartridge bags in the corner, and began to look round to see what there was for lunch, for we were all hungry after being out in the fresh air all the morning. One of the valets spied a large pudding in a basin, standing on the fender in front of the fire. He put it on the table, and began to help it round, observing, "By Jove,

they do us very well here." For it is generally
cold meat and bread for the loaders, sometimes
Irish stew. By the time we were all served, and
were about to begin, the man who was waiting on
the gentry came out of the parlour, and went towards the fireplace. He exclaimed, "Where's the
lark pudding?" He saw it, or what remained of
it, on our table. "Good God," he said, "that pudding was for the Duke of Cambridge." He got a
spoon and scraped it off our plates back into the
basin, and squared it up as best he could. Had
he been a few minutes later there would not have
been any to put back. Lark pudding for servants? What next?

The Duke of Cambridge was the only man who
ever told me I was not holding my gun properly.
We were standing in a sort of ravine waiting. I
had my gun on my shoulder, when I heard a voice
on the rocks above and behind me, shouting, "Put
your gun down, that man there." I looked up.
I did not know any of the guns were stationed
above us. I knew a gun should always be either
pointed to the sky or to the ground by the loader.
I have often thought what a risk some of the bullying sort of gentry (who speak to their servants
worse than they would to a dog, run when out
shooting. When, for instance, a gun might easily
go off "accidently" when climbing through a
hedge, or over a wall. For all loaders do not take

the cartridges out of the gun when doing so, though it is the general rule. A gentleman was once shot in the back by accident, but there is such a thing as "accidently on purpose."

One of the fads this Noble Lord had was when he went out for a walk he would put on four or five overcoats. As his blood began to circulate, and he got warmer, he would take one coat off and throw it down, on the ground or anywhere, and so on further on, till he had only one left. I had to go out afterwards, find out which way he went and collect the coats. If a working man did this sort of thing, people would say he was balmy. But with money in plenty one can do it with impunity. People call it "genious" in an aristocrat, or "originality."

It is not often that, when out shooting, you find a place under cover to eat your lunch in. I remember once when out shooting in Scotland the beer in the bottles froze to a solid mass of ice. They put the bottles between their legs to try and thaw it, but was unable to get any out before we had to begin shooting again. The beef was also so frozen that we could not cut it. It was like a lump of stone.

When the day's shooting is ended the valet takes the guns and cartridges, coats, etc., and gets back to the house as quickly as he can, before his Bos, if possible, in order to get a hot bath ready for him before he arrives.

Once, in Scotland (I did not know the country but could see the house in the distance), I took a bee line across country, thinking it was the nearest way. When within a quarter of a mile I found a river between me and the house, "Well," thinks I, "I'm not going back, I'll try to wade it." I strapped the guns, cartridge bags and coats together, and held them over my head, and went in. Before I got to the middle of the river the water was up under my arms, and still got deeper. I was afraid to go any farther, as I could not attempt to swim under that load; so I turned back and had to go over a bridge half a mile away.

An amusing thing happened where I was staying at a large house in the Eastern Counties. I often used to take a walk round with the head keeper. He told me that a herd of young pigs used to get into the coverts, grubbing about, and disturbing the phesants sitting on their eggs. He had driven them out time after time, but they always came back. When they heard him coming they used to scutter off back to the farm in a drove, down one of the drives in the woods. One day he gave them a dose of sparrow shot out of his gun, at a good distance off. A few days afterwards he was going over the same ground when the farmer asked the keeper if he knew anything about pigs, as all his young ones had developed a lot of pimples on their sterns, a sort of rash had come out; he had never seen anything like it before. The keeper looked at them, said it was very curious, but no doubt would be all right in a day or two.

I had some fine trout fishing while there. I used a worm, which is not considered sportsmanlike, as fly fishing is the correct way to catch trout. When I had caught half a dozen I would take them and grill them for tea. But there was one artful old fellow I could not catch. He used to live among the roots of a tree that the water had washed bare. When he saw me he would simply draw back and wink the other eye, and say, "I don't want your worm." But I had him: he weighed four pounds and a half. I got my worm and rod ready about twenty yards from the bank of the river, then crawled along, laying low, and dropped the line gently into the roots of the tree. He was at home. In an instant the rod was pulled out of my hand; away he went with it. I after him, the end of the rod was sticking out of the water. I waded in and grasped it, and played him till he was tired. In an hour he was on his way to London by parcel post.

This Noble Lord I was with had an idea that I never wanted to go out on my own account. He expected me to be available at any moment of the day or night. When staying at an hotel he would always expect to find me waiting outside his door. I had to get his breakfast ready and wheel it into his room by seven o'clock in the morning. Anyone that has tried this at an hotel knows what that means. If anything was not right to please him, he would send for the manager, and get some of the servants the sack. Those that knew him scuttled out of his way, and spoke of him with awe, in a subdued voice. After two years of this I thought I would try my hand at a butler's job, so I left him.

Nothing would please me at this time but that I should get married. Though whistling, singing, and courting are not allowed in good places, courting is carried on all the same, in a quiet way. Sometimes in the housemaids' cupboard, where they keep their brushes and pails; a few words when passing on the stairs; ways and means can always be found to dodge the housekeeper's eagle eye. Though I must admit it is not plesant or fair to the other servants in the house when courting is going on. But "Love," or Cupid, is such a funny little fellow, and will not be denied. Try to stamp out the flame of love in one place, and it pops up in another. The more one tries to smother it, the fiercer it burns, yet it is said that "Love is blind," if so then his feeling must be exceptionally good, and "eye language" goes a long way with lovers.

Now, for a butler to get married is simply suicidal. Firstly, his employer has got him fairly by the neck. He has got what they call an encumbrance. He cannot move so easily as he could when he was single. They can insult his feelings right and left. He must not answer, or say "Boo to a goose." He has got to console himself with the saying: "It's better to please a fool than tease one." Suppose he is married and takes a place miles in the country; he has taken his wife and furniture, perhaps to live on the estate in a cottage. That man will put up with a great deal before he throws up his place, and has the responsibility of taking his wife and furniture elsewhere, and it is generally "God knows where." On the other hand, should he prove to be unsatisfactory, and he gets the sack, things are blacker still, for he is told: "I have another man coming into the house you occupy on Monday next. So you must get out of it." Perhaps there are no rooms, or a vacant house for miles, but he has to get out. They knew something in the olden days when they only had Eunuchs in their houses to wait on them. No trouble about the butlers' wives and encumbrances then, or courting either. That is why one sees so many advertisements in the papers for "Man and wife." They get them both for the wages of one, and have a stranglehold on them into the bargain. Like the old lady engaging a butler, said she expected him to fill up his spare time in whitewashing, painting, cleaning out the drains, cleaning windows, and feeding and cleaning out the chickens, and take the dogs out for a run. He asked: "Do you keep pigs? Mam." "No," the old lady replied, "not at present." "Then I'm afraid your place won't suit me," replied the butler, "for I am very fond of pigs."

Some years ago I knew of a butler who wished to get married, and asked his employer if he had any objection to his doing so. "No," said his employer, "I have no objection." So accordingly the butler got married, but to his surprise he got a month's notice to leave shortly afterwards. His employer explained that he wanted his butler always within call; but that since he had got married he was often out, as he went home to see his wife, and that his was not "a married butler's place." Taking all things into consideration, a butler ought not to be married. It is not fair to the wife, for she has to mope at home, seeing very little of her husband, while he is at the big house, surrounded with all sorts of womenfolk. The wife remembering that he was somewhat of a "giddy kipper" before he was married, which does not alleviate matters. Should he happen to beget several children, it all goes against them, for the children must not be seen about the place. Of course there are places where a servant is treated as though he were human. There are also some real good places. But the butler stays there, because he cannot better his position by going elsewhere. Supposing by some means I could dislodge him from his position what are the chances that I should get his job? Quite ten thousand to one. But to one good place there are a hundred indifferent ones. Especially since the War, for now the butler has to be the general utility man.

The real good places are nearly always filled, either by promoting the next man that has served under the butler, or by his being known to a branch of the family. An outsider has no chance.

A certain philosopher likens marriage to a man putting his hand into a bag containing a lot of snakes, but only one eel. If he draws out the eel he is lucky. Love is also said to be "blind." It is in a way. For a man does not know everything about a woman, nor the woman everything about a man before they marry. But they find it out afterwards. In the matter of incompability of temper: if they can't find that out before marriage they must fight it out afterwards. It is well known that "Man wants all he can get, and woman wants all she can't get." A man may find himself landed with a partial invalid for life, or "visa versa." This, in the case of a working man, is a great consideration and drawback. Perhaps he finds he is landed on to a woman who can't get up in the morning because she has got a headache. Therefore if he wants any breakfast before he goes to work he must get it ready himself, whether he has a headache or not. A great many women, after marriage, parade these ailments and disabilities to do this or that as an asset, a sort of lawful excuse, so that a man finds instead of a helpmate he has found a hinderance to his making his way through life. To a working man this is serious, but to the gentry it does not matter if his wife stays in bed all day, and every day. The servants will attend to his wants.

I should agree to a law that all persons proposing to marry be thoroughly medically examined, inside and out, and given a certificate. This would prevent a great deal of misery in the world: not only in the case of begetting children, but also in the battle of life.

Well, I got married, which I ought not to have done while my mother was alive. I had saved up the amount of seventy pounds to buy the furniture and launch our boat on the sea of life. Meanwhile things had not gone on well at home. My youngest sister's husband had been playing old gooseberry with things in general. He was out at all hours of the night, and worried my mother to death. In fact she did die shortly after I mar-

ried. I was able to go to her funeral. Thus
ended a hard life, when, with a woman of her education and refinement, her tender disposition and
lovable manner, it ought to have been easier for
her. She had a true sense of religion. As she lay
dieing, the curate called to see her, but she told
him that as she had lived in the same house for
forty years, and he had never called before he
needn't trouble now, it was too late.

Now my sister's husband had to turn too and
work to pay the rent and keep a roof over his
head. They had one child, a girl. They wished
to stay in the house. So I came away and left
them. In the end he got work at Southampton,
on one of the mail boats, through the influence of
a relative of my mother, who held a high position
at the docks. He cleared the house out, and took
all the furniture with him. I did not object as my
sister wanted it for her home, they had no other.
Thus ended the home of my childhood, where I
had spent many happy days. But I myself could
not afford to lose any time. I had little left, except my first-class references, which all showed
that I was a thorough, reliable servant.

I had little trouble in obtaining my first butler's
place, having had such a good schooling in livery.
But it turned out to be more or less a "rotter."
It was situated on the South Coast. I packed my
furniture, and took a cottage near the place, but

not on the estate. I will call the Bos Sir Grizle de Bluster, for he was always on the "nag." The house was an old Elizabethan mansion. The kitchen was like a great barn. Sir Grizel was a typical Member of Parliament, with the brains of a rabbit. It was his money that did it. He made his name famous when he brought in a bill about adding more water to beer, or some such idiotic notion. They had the usual old servant of the family, the housekeeper, to be treated as one of themselves, a trustworthy spy. He also had his old mother to live there with him; she was as deaf as a block. On one occasion the footman ran up to her rooms to tell her the house was falling down. She said, "What?" "The house is falling down, mam." "Goodness gracious, why didn't you tell me before." As the old lady ran out of the room the whole of the five gables fell flat on to the lawn, in one slab, leaving all the insides of the rooms exposed. Which reminds me of an incident that happened at Manchester when I was there. It had been a remarkably wet season. A commercial traveller was occupying a bedroom in an hotel that had recently been built. He had more than a couple of whiskies before retiring. When the side wall of the room fell out, so that the people in the street had a full view of the interior, there he lay in bed. He said he had paid for the room, and he was not going to get up for anybody.

Sir Grizel and the family came to London for
the season. The confidential housekeeper dined in
her own room, at the same time as the family.
When they had finished with the silver dishes in
the dining room, they were taken direct to her
room, from there to the kitchen when she had finished with them. All the other servants dined in
the servants' hall, and got what they could. For
the old confidential used to go out every morning
to either order or bring the things in for the day.
One day she brought some half-ripe plums in late,
and told the cook to make puddings, but as there
was not time, the cook sent in the half-ripe plums
for us to eat as they were in the servants' hall.
"Oh, ours was a nice house, ours was."

When the family returned to the country the
house had been repaired. I thought the circumstances over in my mind. Everything was so different, everything so second rate, that I thought
I could be doing something better. So I gave Sir
Grizel a month's notice. Talk about a whole box
of squibs going off at once! (Sir Grizel stuttered
a bit, especially when he was excited). "What
do you mean? How dare you give me a month's
notice? Come into the billiard room." I followed him in. "Now, what do you mean? How
dare you give me a month's notice?" I said, "I
think I am quite within my rights in doing so."

"Rights! What rights? Talk to me about your rights, I will knock you down with this stick." I said, "I don't think you will, for I am a younger and stronger man than you: if you struck me I should give you such a hiding you would not readily forget." He spluttered, stuttered and foamed at the mouth, and said, "I will send for the police." I said, "I wish you would, for if he is a truthful policeman he will state who struck the first blow. Send for him before you begin knocking me about." Here, then, is a fine illustration of the employer's point of view. This man (I can't call him a gentleman) because he had plenty of money, thought he could have everything he wanted, and no one dare deny him. Everything was quite all right as long as I would take his insults and snubbings without a murmer; but as soon as I had a voice in the matter he went raving mad, and would like to smash me. But he could not compel me to stay in his service. The old slave days have passed away long since. Yet he still thought he had the whip hand of me. He was not compelled to give me a reference, and could bring me to my knees in that way. But he didn't, for I never applied to him for a reference. My previous first-class record would get me a place anywhere. So he found out that there were other things besides "Love" that money would not buy.

Had his constituants known more of his inside life,
he would not have got many votes.   It was simply
the possession of money that did it.

So I put my furniture on the rail, and off we
went back to London town.   I found two nice
rooms at Hampstead, and soon got straight.
Here my son was born, on exactly to the day
twelve months after I was married.   My wife said
she should not do any more travelling about, the
first time sickened her of it.   She said I could get
a place where I liked, but she was going to stay
where she was.   So I scouted round, and got a
situation with a certain Duchess, as butler, but
what a place it turned out to be!   The Duchess
had made herself very unpopular.   There had
been some sort of shady business going on about
the Duke's (her first husband) property.   Eventually she married again, a man beneath her in
rank.   The place had got demoralised.   Butlers
staid only a month, some not that.   So I thought I
would see what I could do with it.   The under
butler was an older man than myself, and had
served the old Duke.   The footmen did just what
they liked, they would not take their turn on duty,
but went out just when they liked.   I tried to lick
them into shape, but they said: "Don't worry
yourself, old chap, you won't be here longer than
the other butlers, about a month."   The husband
had his own valet: he was the spy in the house, in

this case. The Duchess told me he acted as groom of the chambers as well, but when I asked him to take a turn on duty, he said: "Duty be damned. I have got plenty of other work to do beside going on duty." I had to answer all bells, the footmen would only show up when the Duchess was about. They knew her ways. After a short time in London the family went to the country house for a week or so, an enormous place. I went down the day previous to get ready all the writing tables and other things, as the house was to be full of visitors. I went in every bedroom, putting up candles, ink, pens, pencils, notepaper—got lost, and could not find my way back, there was no one about. I ought to have put an envelope on the mat of the door I came in by, as I had to go through a room which was a passage room, before I got to the landing where the staircase was, and the rooms were all alike. The family and guests arrived next day, about twenty of them. In the butler's room was a telephone: all the telegrams were 'phoned from the town, which was ten miles away. That telephone was continuously ringing. I had to copy the message on to an ordinary telegraph form, put it in a buff envelope, address it, then diliver it. By the time I got back three or four other messages were waiting to be taken off. There was quite enough telephone work for one person. However, I struggled through somehow.

The gentry played cards until two and three in the morning, and they were a thirsty lot. The Duchess would hold a sort of levee in her boudoir every morning. First I got my whigging, then the head gardener, coachman, keeper—she had them all in. She always said I never washed out her fountain pens every morning. It was useless my saying I had done them. One morning she came into her boudior dressed in a white muslin dress, trimmed with blue bows and ribbons. She began about the pens, took hold of one, tugged it open: the ink went all over the front of her dress. I was glad to beat a retreat, as she ran into her bedroom. Not being popular with the families in the highest circles, the Duchess and her beloved spouse had to put up with the second-raters, comprising theatrical people, and such like, a lot of people on the look out for something for nothing. The servants were constantly changing. Those leaving they sent away by a different line and station from those new ones arriving, so that they should not meet. One day they did meet, at the Junction, all the jolly lot went back to London together, the new ones and the old. Eventually we returned to the London house, where they gave a large dinner party. They were a thirsty lot. On these occasions the valet had to help wait at table. As soon as I filled their glasses with champayne, they picked them up and emptied them at one gulp. The Bos, seeing the glasses empty, told me to hand the wine, with the same result as before. The next morning the Bos asked me how many bottles of champayne were used for the dinner party. I told him. He said, "Impossible." Then he said he had been told that the men who carried up the dinner was seen to be drinking champayne in the serving room. That was not true, for they did not get the chance. What the valet did see was the men sucking at the empty bottles, for I left nothing in them: there may have been a few drops left in the bottom of the bottles. He stormed and fumed. I told him I did not want his champayne or him either. I asked him to give me my wages, and I would clear out at once. The footmen were right. I was only there about a month, and that was a month too long. After that they told the under butler if he did not accept the butler's place, he would have to leave. He had been offered the place on previous occasions, but knew better than accept it. Anyhow, he took the place. Shortly after he could not be found. Eventually they found he was in his room, locked in, and as drunk as a lord. The Duchess was frightened to death he would set the house alight.

CHAPTER IX

THERE are plenty of good footmen that make very
bad butlers: they are all right as long as they wear
the buttons, but when they don the black coat, and
have men under them, they are all at sea. They
find they have to see that the other men do their
work properly; if he rebukes them he has to take
their insults, for they know he has not the power
to discharge them. He is supposed to drive, but
his Master holds the whip. If he reports a few
of them, and get them discharged as unsuitable,
he is quickly told that he does not know how to
manage his men: that he is too hard on them. The
butler has not the same position as a sergeant in
the army, where the officers uphold any reasonable
complaint, but the butler must by his own person-
ality control his men, or they will pretty soon control him. Besides this there is another consideration in favour of the footmen: that is, the liveries.
If a man leaves after short service all his liveries
has to be either renewed or altered. I will state
a case in point. The family I was with had taken
the house of the Duke of —— in an Eastern
County. The two footmen were inclined to resent
all authority, and wanting to do what they liked

and leave the rest to the butler. At night they
could not be found when the house was shut up
for the night, but they found some means of getting into the house after it was closed, notwithstanding. At first I had to sit up to let them in.
They would bolt off to the pub in the village, and
remain there till closing time, and after. I always gave my men one chance, and told them they
must get in to time; and that I should not wait up
to let them in. I found they got in by leaving their
bedroom window open, which was on the ground
floor. They simply ignored me. So I fastened
their window, and went to bed. A policeman always patrolled round the house at night. In case
of an alarm, he could ring a bell in my bedroom
from outside, which was also on the ground floor.
That night at 12.30 the bell rang. The two footmen and the policeman stood outside the window.
I said, "Hullo, what do you want?" They said,
"We want to come in." I said, "Then you can
damn well stop out." The family had gone to
Scotland for a fortnight the day before.

The next morning the footmen started a row:
wanted to fight me. I said, "Right ho, I'll take
you on one at a time, and I'll give you the dam'dest
hiding you ever had in your life." When they saw
I meant business, they climed down, but thinks I,
"This is the final; either they leave, or I get out
of it myself." I at once sent a telegram to the

Bos. In an hour or so the reply came: "Pay footmen, and send them off by next train." Here, then, is the instance of the butler being expected to drive, and having to wire to the Bos to apply the whip, or put on necessary pressure to keep order.

Sometimes the butler rows in with those under him, but that game can't last long, for what is the use of a butler who does not aim at discipline, and order in a house, and who is not to be trusted to take care of property and things placed under his charge? If there is no order kept in a house there is no comfort for anybody. Not overlooking the possibility of a burglary through a house not being properly locked up at night. In that event, the footmen who left the window open would not be blamed. It would be the butler's fault for not seeing the house properly locked up. There is where the footmens' laugh comes in. But the outcome of this affair did not altogether rest with me. There are always spies about a place who tittle-tattle to the Master or Mistress, everything they see or hear amongst the other servants. Someone would have seen them out at that time of night, after the house should have been locked up for the night. The news would quickly travel, and a butler would be brought to book for allowing it, and be told he was not trustworthy. No matter what the butler has to say by way of de-

fending or explaining himself his employer will
believe only what it suits him to believe. Every
household is carried on in this despotic fashion.
Servants are treated as though they are the employer's personal property, to be able to make, or
break, as they think fit, and which they are able to
do, by means of the servant's "character." They
are servants by name, but slaves in everything but
the name. For as the poet saith:—

"A man's a fool who strives by force or skill
To stem the torrent of a woman's will,
For if she will, she will, you may depend on't,
And if she won't, she wont, so there's an end on't."

Every man, from the King downwards, knows
secretly in his heart that his wife is the "King of
the Castle." He may bluster and "Swank" as
much as he likes, but he has to give way in the
end. If he does not she can make things so
darned uncomfortable, that he wishes he had never
been born, or he gets a divorce. That is why
I think there is such a lot in Physchic Auto-
suggestion. A clever conversationalist, either a
man or woman, may put things in such a way that
one may be made to think things against one's will.
Simply twist them round with their fingers, so to
speak.

The greater the number of friends the gentry
have, the more popular they think they are, and

get a paragraph in the daily papers about what they do, and what they don't do. Of course those with most money will have most friends to come and eat at their table, and sponge on them generally. If they went to an hotel to lunch or dinner they would have to pay for the service, one way or another. But when they come to lunch or dine, or stay on a visit, they get it all gratis. The extra service being included in the butler's wages. They make no end of extra work, but no matter how much is piled on him he gets no extra pay for doing it.

I remember a case in point, that happened in Pont Street some few years ago. The butler and footman had prepared for the usual members of the family for lunch. As they were about to sit down in troops three extra ladies: come to lunch, of course. The old lady, the hostess, was a bit deaf, she shrieked out, "Perkins, you have not laid any places." He asked her if she knew these people were coming to lunch. She replied, "Yes, of course, and I told the cook. He said, "The cook don't lay the cloth." So that proves that she expected (like a great many more of them) that the butler should work under the cook's orders. Nice position, ain't it?

Obviously, all these gentrys' friends and visitors cannot be unmarried. They hold the marriage rights very lightly, as told by the Divorce Court, but how much of it happens that is never published, or even found out? They take all these happenings as a matter of course. For what have they got to do with their time, day after day? When ordinary pleasure wanes and pals on them, they go farther and farther, until it gets too hot, then there is a "bust up" and out it all comes in the Divorse Court.

I was once collecting the letters for post in a very large house, when I saw something of the sort. It is not usual to knock the doors before entering the living rooms in large places, excepting perhaps "My Ladies Boudoir," and, of course, bed rooms. I had collected some letters, then went on to the library (for woe betide the butler who does not collect them all, especially in a country place with only one post out a day). I opened the door, but shut it again very quickly and quietly, for what I saw was not a sight fit for curates. The Noble Earl's back was towards the door, but the lady visitors was not. Yet, there was the Noble Earl's wife in her boudoir, innocently writing letters, some distance away, unconscious of it all. But I will relate nothing more of what I saw. I will here pull down the blind. I thought to myself, "Letters, or no letters, I am not going in that room again." Some people would imagine a servant would have some sort of pull or advantage in such a case as this: but such is not the case. If they even suspected that a servant knew, or saw something of the sort, some excuse would soon be found for getting rid of him, and what weight would a servant's word be against theirs? It would pay a servant better to keep his mouth shut about it. But when I hear, or read in the newspapers, that a servant has been left a good round sum of money in a will, I always imagine there has been some dirty work somewhere, and the servant knew it. Maybe, the rightful heir had at some time been done out of his rights. Or foul play may have been employed, such as poison, or many other ways. It is pretty certain he does not get it because of his pure slogging work.

I was nearly getting £500 once, but that was for doing, or trying to do something. But as "A miss is as good as a mile" I may as well relate the story. A story of drink.

I had engaged myself as butler-valet to a young married gentleman, very rich, and a brother to a great friend of the late King Edward.

I had only been there a few days, when I found out where the trouble was. He had married a young woman far beneath him, in fact, a tradesman's daughter; and like a great many more of young men of good family, who marry actresses, chorus girls, and such like, simply spoil their lives. They are driven off their balance by a pretty face;

but whose knowledge of housekeeping, or managing a house, extends as far as a restaurant table, where they have been taken by so called gentlemen. Sometimes their married life lasts only a short time. In others they live in the same house but each go their own way in life, being afraid of scandal. This particular woman was as pretty as a wax doll, small of stature, with golden hair, of Scotch extraction, but she had an awful temper. She was everlasting nagging her husband. He must have been drunk when he married her. Like the parson who refused to marry a certain couple because the man was so drunk. "Well, sir," said the would be bride, "I can't get him to come when he is sober."

One night at dinner the soup did not please him. What he called it I will not relate. He took the soup tureen, and threw tureen and all on the fire. The little lady blamed me for allowing him to get the drink, whereas he was "Tishy" when he came in from his club. I refused to have anything to do with the wine cellar keys, and gave them up to her. Shortly afterwards he wanted whiskey. I told him I had not got the cellar keys, and that his wife had them. As she would not hand them over he came down to the basement, got an axe, and split the wine cellar door to pieces, made a hole large enough for a man to get through, and told me to get out a bottle of whiskey. Lord,

how I pittied that man.   He was like a great good
tempered schoolboy when he was sober.   He could
see that he had ruined his life by marrying this
woman.   He could not take her into Society for
her Scotch brogue was that hard one could almost
cut it with a knife.

I tried the process of giving him his whisky and
soda a little weaker every time, till at last he would
say: "I asked you for whiskey, not plain soda
water," and would then pitch glass and all under
the grate.   Sometimes in this way I would get him
nearly sober, and he would talk sensibly.

One day he asked me if I was going to stick to
gentleman's service all my life.   I said my object
was to save enough to take a little business of some
sort.   He asked, "About how much would you
want to make a start?"   I replied, "I ought to
make a decent start with five hundred pounds."

"Well," he said, "as you seem to be the only
one who cares anything about me, if you stick to
me you shall have it."   For when he was sober I
used to try and persuade him to keep away from
the drink.   I could see he was sorry for himself,
and wished he could.   He would then give me a
few cigars.   But he was weak, both in will power
and in determination to resist it.   For he would
go off to his club and all my work was undone.
A man with so much money to spend did not lack
friends galore—of a sort.   Some of them were

just sharks, who used to cheat him at cards. He had a sailing yacht, and we used to go yacht-racing at Cowes, Oban, and the Clyde. On one occasion, when playing cards on the yacht, he was not so drunk as they thought him to be, when he detected one of the players (a certain Captain in the Army) cheating. He took all the cards and threw them overboard, and said he would not allow another card on his yacht. In this he kept his word. He kept a chef and a steward aboard, and the same crew came with him every yachting season, for when sober he was a perfect gentleman, but simply helpless when drunk. I can picture him now, having his hair cut on deck, with the "Union Jack" to cover him.

I used to like getting up in the early morning to go ashore with the chef and steward to buy provisions at the early markets. It was life indeed, cruising on the West Coast of Scotland. One morning I was nearly knocked overboard. The mate let go the jib sail when tacking: it caught me. He did not know I was up "forrard," and he could not see me where he stood.

The Bos took a large house in Argyleshire, with a grouse moor, and fishing. He filled the house with his "friends," and they spent their time in shooting, yachting, and fishing, also plenty of card playing. He lent me a gun and I had a fine time with the rabbits. The life on the moors did him a lot of good: he kept fairly sober. London was the very worst place for him.

One day he invited every man who had, or could carry a gun, from the town and country round about to a day's shooting of white hares. (At a certain time of the year in Scotland the hares turn quite white.) About fifty of us started. We formed a ring round the foot of a high mountain, and gradually drove them towards the top, where there promiced to be some lively shooting. Most of the men understood nothing of the rules of shooting. The guns were pretty thick on top, and I often had to lie flat on the heather and be fired over, for guns pointed at one from all directions. However, the affair passed off without any accident. Everybody enjoyed themselves, for there was no lack of food and whiskey. Every man having some game to take home with him.

Most of the crew of the yacht were single men, only the Captain being married. One day the Bos asked them why they did not marry. He said:— "Fifty pounds to the one who marries first." The mate was not long about it, and got the fifty pounds. "Thirty pounds for the next," he said. That was soon claimed. Twenty-five pounds he gave each to the rest of the crew when they married.

One night I was just about to serve dinner at the house. I was getting some soda water out of

the cellarette in the sideboard, when one exploded
in my hand, like a Mill's bomb. It split my hand
about five inches. One could see the white liga-
ments that work the fingers; luckily none of these
were cut, or it would have stopped my violin playing for ever, being the left hand. The Bos put
me in a pony cart, I was taken to a doctor several
miles away. I tried not to faint, but had to
against my will. The doctor put eight stitches in
my hand. Eventually it got quite allright, except
the marks.

A curious incident happened while we were
there. I had a footman who had "Religious
mania." That is all right within limits, but one
never knew where he was. He neglected his work.
I could seldom find him, so I had to do his work
myself. I found that he went into the town, got
on a soap box, and preached to those who chose to
listen to him. But it did not end there. He
would get a crowd of them to come up to the house,
and hold prayer meetings in his bedroom, which
was on the ground floor; afterwards giving them
all supper in the servants' hall. The cook complained to me, and said she could not feed all that
crowd, for two legs of mutton quickly disappeared,
and he came for more. I spoke to him about it,
also about neglecting his work. Work was the
last of his thoughts. Religion was never meant to
throw one off their mental balance. Neither is it

religion simply to call oneself a Christian, and say you are of the Church of England, or any other church. Religion is shown in our actions of every day of our lives, in practical sympathy, in helping the needful, in unselfishness, in going out of our way, if need be, to help others not so well off in this world's goods as ourselves. Not doing it to the accompanyment of a blare of trumpets, in order to get our names published in the newspapers. As to going to church. How many ladies would go if the new dress or new hat or toque they expected had not arrived. Mrs. Lauds Struth had a new toque arrive, Mrs. Bron Kitis (anybody above a tradesman has a double-barrelled name) expected a new hat which had not arrived. Consequently Mrs. Bron Kitis does not go to church. If she did shafts of envy would be flying about, like wireless, though both of them may consider themselves good Christians.

But to revert to our Bible-thumper. I told him what he did when he was off duty had nothing to do with me, but he was not to have prayer meetings at the house, and that the suppers would be stopped. His bedroom was on the ground floor, close to the back entrance. One night, soon afterwards, the cook told me they were all trooping in as usual. I thought something must be done.

I said to the cook, "Leave it to me, I'll soon shift them." I put a fire-shovel in the fire till it

was red hot, then just before I pushed it under
his door, where the stones were worn, I sprinkled
a little cayenne pepper on the shovel, let it remain
a second under the door, took it out, and disappeared to watch events. Soon they all came rushing out into the courtyard, sneezing one against
the other like mad. I asked the footman what
was the matter? Had his Satanic Majesty been
whisking his tail round about? Though this appeared to me to be approaching a mean action, I
found that nothing else would move them, as
serious diseases require serious remedies. It was
far from my thoughts to ridicule religion. It was
mostly for a "lark." His audiance must have
thought it a very good religion, with a good supper
to follow at somebody else's expense. As the footman got worse and more dazed every day I was
obliged to report the matter, as he was no use to
me. So the Bos sent the poor fellow back to London, where, no doubt, he may be seen in Hyde
Park, on a soap box, holding forth to his heart's
content.

Writing about soap boxes reminds me of the
attempt by some wild scallywags to form a "Servants' Union." What a farce. As though they
could make the gentry do anything they did not
want to do! They would simply laugh in derision.
Why, if every British servant came out they could
easily fill their places with foreigners, and much

cheaper, too.   Failing that, they could live at hotels.   Dictate to the gentry, what ho!   What next?

And if they could only perswade a man to go on strike and leave a good place, the fellow on the soap-box would jump down and rush off as fast as he could to see if he could get the place the fellow had come out of.

They need not worry themselves.   The gentry have got the servants by the neck right enough. When they are served by the best servants in the land they are just the same.   They don't forget to let you know on every possible occasion that you are a servant.   They have a stranglehold on the liberty of the subject.   The only thing is, if the servant objects to the long hours of work, and every hour of the day or night, if required, to get out of it altogether, and try some other profession.

Mention was made of an eight hour day's work for servants.   I myself have worked for sixteen hours a day continously, so that would just be half a day's work.   The employers would halve the wages, half to the first shift, and half to the second shift.   So that although the servants would get more liberty they would have very little money in their pockets to spend, and having no home handy they must go under cover somewhere in wet or bad weather.   Though a great many maid-servants are taken from so called homes for training them, they do not want them there after they have been launched off into service.

But I must get aboard the yacht again. The Bos kept comparatively sober for a time. We won one or two races. On the occasion of a win it was an excuse for him to break out again. Any fool can get drunk, but it takes a man to get sober.

Under the seats were lockers in the floors of the cabin, by lifting up a strip of carpet were baths. All these, and every available place were cram full of bottles of whiskey, champayne, and all sorts of wines and liqueurs. I think we were at Oban. The Bos was so bad, and could not recover himself, but laid in his bunk for days, till eventually we had to send ashore for a doctor. The doctor immediately ordered all the wines and spirits to be taken ashore in the boats, every bottle to be stored there. Otherwise, he said he would not be answerable for the Bos' life. It took a week for the doctor to bring him to himself again.

How sorry I was that a nice young gentleman should get in such a state. When the yachting season was over the yacht was laid up, and we returned to London. Here we were in the danger zone again. For the Bos would naturally go to his club for he could get no rest or comfort at home. His wife was continually nagging him, when all the time he required tender persuasion. I often had to go to his club at night and bring

him home in a hansom cab (for there were no taxis
in those days). I would find him "all of a heap"
in a big arm chair, before the fire, "dead to the
world." I would get him home, and to bed. In
the morning I would try him with some good
strong soup, to get a foundation to his stomach,
but he would seldom drink it. All he wanted was
whiskey and soda. After a bit I would get him
downstairs and talk nicely to him, trying to persuade him to make a stand against the drink. He
would not drink cocoa, for it is an excellent thing
when a man is in such a state and finds the craving
for drink coming on, to take copious drinks of
cocoa; of course a certain amount of determination is required, which he had not. Towards the
afternoon, being young he had recouperated a bit,
and was very thankful to me for taking such care
of him, but at night he would dress for dinner,
and go to his club. He seldom dined with his
wife. If he did it was like a wild beast show, and
ended up in a quarrel: she had no tact. At the
club he met his "friends," and all my work was
undone again. If he did not arrive home by
eleven o'clock I had to go again and bring him
home, and go through the same process again. It
was only natural that this could not continue for
long without a breakdown. It came. The doctor
was called in. After a time the doctor ordered
him to take a tour abroad, in order to get away

from it all, especially his "friends." Though he took drink to obtain oblivion from his miseries, they returned tenfold in the morning. So we packed up, and set off for the South of France.

CHAPTER X

My slender practical railway experience I always found useful in all my travels. We staid a week at one of the best hotels in Paris. Here I explored a bit, endeavouring to find my way about, and to see the sights, and as I could not speak but a few words of the language I often got lost. From thense we went on via Lyons to Cologne and Frankfort, to Pau and Bairretz; through miles and miles of pine forests, the trees each with their little pail attached to catch the turpentine. We remained at Pau two months, where I learnt enough of the language to ask for things I wanted. Then on to Antwerp and Birkenhammer where they make such beautiful glass. Though I enjoyed the trip I cannot say I enjoyed the food, so different from the substantial English fare.

What I missed a lot was the tea. It is usual for ladiesmaids and valets to take the tea from England and form a five o'clock tea-party in one of their own rooms. The Bos saw us one day through his window across the courtyard. He asked who the party were. I said one of the maids was the one who darned his socks (as we took no ladies maid with us). He put his hand in his

pocket and threw two Louis on the table and said,
"Take her to the Circus to-night." I often had
to search for him at night, though he was not so
bad as when in London. I had one of his cards,
and could get into the Casino. I started out to
walk to the Pyrinees Mountains one afternoon.
They looked about ten miles off, with their snow-
covered tops, and was surprised when they were
sixty miles away. I passed a French Infantry
Regiment with their red trowsers and blue coats,
who were on the march, so that my walk was not
in vain.

Eventually the time came for our return to
London. The Bos certainly looked better, and
was twice the man he was when we went away.
But, alas, the first time he went to his club he was
as bad as ever. Quarelling began again, till one
day he told me to pack some things, as he was
going to sleep at his Club. I was to go and call
him each morning. The first morning everything
was all right: that was on a Saturday. The next
morning I went to his room. He was not there,
neither had he been there that night. He had
changed into evening dress clothes and gone out.
Here was a pretty pickle. Where should I go to
look for him? I knew there were several warm
places round about Leicester Square, where some
of the "lively sparks" might have got hold of him.
Which way should I go? That's the question, as

it was getting on for eleven o'clock. Just then I
saw him turn the corner of the street in a hansom
cab. He sat back in one corner, his silk hat all
ruffeled up, his white tie was under his ear. He
did look a spectacle. If it was not for the tragedy
of the thing I might say comical; and all the
people just going to Church. I soon got him out,
and up to his room, undressed and put him to
bed. In his pockets were all sorts of funny things,
which showed where he had been; but no money.
They had skinned him out clean.

When he woke up I asked him where his gold
watch and chain was, thinking he had lost that
as well. But he had the sense to leave that behind
overnight, locked in a drawer of the dressing table.
"Well," I thought, "this is a deplorable state of
affairs. Oh, if I could only do something to stop
his craving for drink."

In the evening his wife was walking up and
down outside the club, waiting for him to come
out, which eventually he did. She persuaded him
to go home. I got them a hansom cab, and
followed in another shortly afterwards, when I had
collected and packed his things. When I arrived
at the house I was surprised to see a crowd round
the door, and a Police Sergeant and a Constable
inside. What had happened is this:—When the
cab arrived at his house and he saw where he was
he did not want to go in. His wife had got out

of the cab to open the door, or ring the bell. The
Bos grabbed the reins that were over his head, the
driver up at the back tugged to recover possesion
of them, the consequence was, the horse bolted
down the street at full gallop, collided with a
refuge in the middle of the street, overturned the
cab, and there was a general smash up. The
police were quickly on the scene, and the Bos
would have been taken to the police station or hospital had not the coachman's wife happened to be
passing at the time, and told the policeman who
he was.

Beyond a slight cut on the forehead from broken
glass, and a shaking, he appeared to have escaped
injury. It is curious how seldom a drunken man
injures himself when falling about. The Bos sat
in a chair, and after a few formalities the police-
men were satisfied, also the cabman, who escaped
injury. The crowd soon scattered, and all was
again quiet. We got the Bos to bed, sent for a
doctor, who sent medicine, and gave orders that
he was not to have anything intoxicating in any
shape or form. He fell into a deep sleep, from
the effect of what the doctor gave him. When he
woke up he rang the bell. I went up, and was
surprised to find the door was locked, and the key
gone. He was shouting my name, but his wife
would not give me the key, or unlock the door.
So I could do nothing. He remained like this for

a few days, continually shouting for me, but his
wife would not let me go in to him. The next
morning he was dead, and so was the five hundred
pounds that he had promiced that I should have.
For I had nothing in writing to show, neither was
it mentioned in his will.

I had no idea the end was so near, but outraged
human nature could not stand such treatment any
longer. He died at the age of twenty-eight, who,
under favourable circumstances, would have enjoyed a long life. With plenty of money, and
everything one could wish for in this world, excepting a suitable, loving wife. The Bos could
not take her amongst his friends, and she could not
pull him down to her own level. Thus ended that
tragedy. How many similar marriages are there
in Britain, in the present day, when scoins of
Noble houses have taken to marrying chorus girls
off the stage because they have a pretty face?
Very few of them turn out a success. After the
first glamour has worn off they scuttle off to the
Divorse Court.

After the funeral the house and everything was
sold, servants paid off and discharged. The
goldenhaired, doll-faced little widow went back
amongst her own set again; well provided for, of
course. The best place for her.

The Bos was a gentleman, who, if he could have
had the courage and will to resist drink, I could

have served all the days of my life; but his wife
I would not serve willingly for five minutes. She
had made a good shot, and had made sure of a
fortune for life, but had ruined a life in the
process. What a thing for her to look back upon;
though I firmly believe half the gentry have no
conscience whatever, or smother it, knowing
"Conscience maketh cowards of us all."   Drink
is a proper curse, if used to excess. I once heard
of a butler who had a peppermint in his speech.
Now, anyone with an impediment in his speech
is useless as a servant. This particular butler was
fond of a nip of whiskey "Little and often."
When he answered the bells he popped a pepper-
ment in his mouth to take away the smell of the
whiskey. I suppose the Bos had other evidence
of his drinking habits. So gave him notice to
leave, saying he had had enough of it, and his
"damned peppermints also." An old boozer once
had a dream of a real El Dorado. He dreamt
that he and his palls was swimming down a river
of ale. He enjoyed this immensely. Later on he
came to an island; on this island was a spring, not
of water but of whiskey. He shouted to his pals:
"Chaps, throw away your little half pint mugs
and hurry up with your quart cans." Then he
woke up.

While we are on a "wet" subject, I may as well
relate one or two more incidents. Some years

ago, before electric light was in use, the living rooms were lighted by wax candles, occasionally by Moderator lamps, which burnt colza oil. A butler to a Noble Lord was fond of a drop of whiskey (I knew him personally). He lived in Portman Square. On several occasions her Ladyship had told him not to stand on the drawing room chairs and sofas to light the candles in the sconces. Dinner being over, he rushed up to the drawing room to "light up." The ladies left the dining room sooner than he expected. He stood on a sofa that crossed the corner of the room. He had taken a drop or two extra that night. As the ladies came in at the door he lost his balance and toppled over the back of the sofa into the corner. "Tableau." Another butler was so "Tishy" that, on answering a bell, he got into the middle of the drawing room, and after receiving the order, had lost all sense of direction as to where the door was. He started going, but entirely in the wrong direction, and ended up by falling under a table in the corner opposite the door. The lady rang the bell again, and told the footman to take the butler away. I heard the lady relate the above story.

But those hard-drinking days are long past. Even the servants' beer is not allowed, whereas, in former days, it was to be found in most houses in plenty, now, if one can get a cup of cocoa extra one is lucky. It is no exaggeration in saying that gentleman's service has "gone to the dogs." All "Esprit de Corps" of the profession died years ago. In olden times visitors would be as much surprised to see the house gone, as not to see the old butler there. He was a familiar part of the concern. It would not seem like the same place if he was not there. A fine, plump, old fellow, with a self-satisfied smile on his face, and a smile of welcome for you. What do you see now-a-days? A fellow with a look on his face that one would expect to see on the face of a hunted fox, or other animal. Pale and emetic, and wishes he had never been born, to have to cope with these hurry-scurry, tear away days. Days that are not half long enough for his employer's pleasures—jazzing, card playing, theatres and pictures, dinner parties. But they are careful to see that servants has no time for any of these pleasures.

.   .   .   .

In all these years I had very little chance of seeing much of my wife and boy. For gentleman's service is such that one never knows where the wind of circumstances is going to waft one next. North, East, South or West. Excepting when I was out of place was I able to stay with them. They had moved from Hampstead to her native place in Surrey, where she had relations, and was better known.

My brother, the partner of most of my youthful escapades, came South to London.   His Bos took a fancy to him after two years as footman, and put him in his office in the city, where he staid seven years: then he took a business in London and got married.   After twenty years of business he wanted a more outdoor life.   So he bought a new taxi for five hundred pounds, passed Scotland Yard examinations, and got to work.   I mention these things as some of them come into the picture later on.   My brother had had enough of gentleman's service.   He saw where it led to, in time.

Well, here I was on the pavement again, looking for a job, with very little money in my pocket, as I had to send nearly all my wages home.   I had lost touch with nearly all my former acquaintances through whom I was likely to hear of a situation vacant, and registry offices I abhor.   So I put an advertisement in the *Morning Post,* and got several replies.   One was to meet a titled lady, who lived just this side of Portsmouth, so I started off to see her.

On my arrival at the little station I think I was the only passenger who got out.   I noticed a lady coming towards me.   She asked my name, and said she was the lady I had come to see.   I noticed her carriage was outside the station.   My suspicions were at once aroused.   Why had she come to the station to meet me?   Was it so that

I should not have any chance to talk to any of her servants at the house? Anyhow, I thought so. We went into the little waiting room, eyeing each other like two expert swordsmen. After a deal of chin wagging I told her I would decide, and let her know on the following morning. I was not so rude as to tell her to her face that her place would not suit me, but I wrote her a letter saying so. I heard afterwards that the place was "hot."

But one cannot always tell the outcome of these sort of interviews. For, on again advertising, a gentleman wished me to go and see him at an hotel at Crewe Station, stating he would pay my fare. I went, and saw him and his lady. They seemed fair and straightforward, so I accepted the position. On my arrival at the station nearest their house by train appointed, the porter said, "Are you going up to the Hall? (For there is something about a servant that one can always surmise the fact). I said, "Yes." He replied, "You have got the best place in Homeshire." Thinks I, "This sounds a bit encouraging." But I eyed him keenly to see if he was joking. The proof of a pudding is the eating thereof. No matter how brightly a place is painted, one cannot tell untill a week or two has passed as to what it really is like, for they are all different. Your methods may not be their methods, and one has to quickly adapt oneself to their ways. For it is the em-

ployers who pay the piper, and expect everything
done as they wish. That is the advantage of experience, to be able to do things any way and every
way.

I may safely say that this was the best situation
I ever had, though not the largest, as there were
only seven men kept in the house. Everything
about the place was first-class, and kept in first-
class order. The Bos was a real gentleman of the
old school. He had been Colonel in the Guards,
so that he knew what men were, that they were
made of flesh and blood, human beings, and not
mere machines. Everyone who came to the house
with a parcel, message, note or what not, were en-
titled to a pint of beer, also bread and cheese.
I had an office, a nice little room, near the back
entrance, for I had to keep all household accounts,
wine cellar books, and accounts of all petty expences. This used to be the meeting place of the
clerk of the works, head gamekeeper, head gardener, and head coachman, for half an hour before
dressing for dinner. Here we used to have a
friendly chat, and tell the latest "Bon Mot," and
talk of the events of the day, and what was likely
to happen on the morrow. There was no stint of
a glass of beer, or perhaps a nip of whiskey. For
the Bos liked his servants to be happy and comfortable. The Bos was a fine old sportsman of
the first class: had good phesant and partridge

shooting on his estate. Everyone liked him; though a keen disciplarian, he would stand no nonsence. No use trying hoodwink him. He could detect the false from the true in an instant. The footmen wore smart liveries. Chocolate coloured coats, with red collars and cuffs, scarlet waistcoats and breeches, all trimmed with silver brade, pink silk stockings, buckled shoes, powdered hair when we had visitors, and when at the London house. All the servants were happy enough at this place, though we had to work very hard at times, and for many hours a day: still, there were slack times when I used to give them a dance in the servants' hall, which was something for them to look forward to. Even down to the scullerymaid, for she knew it was a foundation for better positions. For any of the best families in the land would take a servant from such a place as that. To know that they had served there was recommendation enough. The place was sort of self-contained, for in a road that led down to the back carriage drive, was blacksmith, carpenter's, bricklayer's, and painter's shops, and a stone mason's yard. So that all repairs, building required, also on the farms on the estate, was done by his own men. The Bos was very fond of cricket, and had a splendid ground and permanent cricket pavilion, where sixty could sit down to luncheon at one time. All the china and glass were kept in a pantry there,

opposite which was a kitchen for dishing up the
food.   At the back was a copper for hot water,
the small plate and knives were the only things
brought to the house after the cricket match was
over.   All the washing up was done there.   On
these occasions the Bos would playfully shake his
fist in my face and say: "You have got something to do for the next fortnight.   Don't you
dare to run short of anything!"   It would be my
fault if there was not plenty of everything, for
I had a free hand, to order what was wanted.   The
house was crammed full of visitors.   I got in eight
extra waiters, they with our own staff made fifteen
men, beside that there were several visiting valets.
So for that fortnight I had to use my wits to keep
everything going.   The ladies used to come to the
house from the cricket ground to lunch, generally
about thirty.   We had fifty to dinner every night.
County cricket teams used to play.   Gentry came
with their parties from miles round: it was a great
social event.

Burgundy cup, Champayne cup, Moselle cup
were in great demand all day.   A donkey cart
was constantly going backwards and forwards
(about a quarter of a mile) for fresh supplies.
The head waiter would write on a piece of paper
whatever he was running short of.   I would pack
it in the cart, and send it up to him.   I and the
footmen staid at the house to prepare for the din-

ner at night. Our own valet was a very smart-
looking man. He had been in the Life Guards.
Over six feet high, black hair, slim, he looked a
perfect gentleman when dressed: a good-tempered,
nice, jolly fellow, always open for a joke or a bit
of fun. He used to say the stuff was never yet
brewed that would make him drunk. But I had
"ma doots." I have lived with three valets who
were ex-Life Guardsmen. The amount of beer
those fellows could put away was astonishing; and
it did not seem to have any more effect on them
than a fly on an elephant's back. But drinking
spirits was bound to have effect if persisted in.
Every year eight gallons of whiskey came from
Scotland to fill up the thirty gallon barrel, which
had not been empty for twenty-five years, so that
some of it was pretty old stuff. One day when I
was filling the barrel up, the fumes went all over
the place. The valet got scent of it, and followed
the trail, till he came to the little square grating
in the cellar door, which I had taken the precaution
to lock on the inside. He wanted to come in, but
for his own good I said, "No, I will give you a
glass before you go to bed." For if I had let him
in I should not have been able to get him out, and
I should have been sorry if anything happened to
him through me.

The Bos was "great" at shooting lunches; in
fact, from a sportsman's point of view, too elabor-

ate.   In every case we had to provide it just the
same as in the dining room, whether it be in a farm
house, a barn, or woodman's hut.   The clerk of
the works got his orders at our usual "session"
overnight, as to how many there would be.   He
and his men would fix up the tables all ready, also
a stove alight.   I had to get all the table appoint-
ments, food and drinks, cigars and cigarettes, together, and drive, with the valet and steward's
room boy to wait on them.   Often all the ladies
would come out to the shooting lunch, when they
would number five and twenty.   All the hot joints
and other food were put in bright copper pans
with lids.   We could hear when they were getting
near by the sound of the guns; then we began to
"dish up."

On one of these occasions the valet took the Bos'
shooting cap (an old greasy cap.   He said he
could not shoot straight in any other, though he
had a dozen) and hung it on the elbow of the stove
pipe to dry.   About the time we were handing the
coffee a most undescribable smell pervaded the
place, something like burning, oily rag, scented.

When we got behind the screen we saw the cap
just about to catch alight, with a hole burnt
through the top.   The valet was in a fix.   It was
too far to send the boy to the house on his bycicle
to get another cap in time.   We watched the valet
through the cracks of the screen when he took the

cap to the Bos and handed it to him. "Look," said the Bos to the company, "what they have done to my cap! They would burn me, if they dared."

Yes, he was a grand old gentleman: his like will never be seen again. When he travelled people would walk along the train and look at him, for he had a striking resemblance to the late King Edward. The people often thought it was the King, and ask the valet if it was so.

The head coachman was an exceedingly smart little man. The way he and his men turned his horses, carriages, and four in hand, was beyond compare. We always had a house full for the Chester and Manchester race meetings, comprising not a few owners of race horses. On one occasion the coachman was very keen on getting information respecting a particular race. During dinner little was said about racing during the conversation. They reserved that untill the ladies and servants had left the room, discussing it over the "Nuts and wine."

The little coachman got some of the others to pull him up in the dinner lift, which opened out into the dining room, behind a large screen. There he remained in that cramped position untill he got the information he wanted. Everyone had a very profitable day at the races the next day, for the horse came in first.

While at the races I was standing close to a

bookmaker, when an old farmer came up, and put a sovereign on an outsider at 25 to 1. The bookie and his clerk smiled at the old fellow. The race started with shouts of "They're off." The horse the old farmer had backed kept creeping on, passing the others, one by one, untill at the "distance" there was only that and the favourite "in it." However, the farmer's choice got beaten by a short head. The farmer said, "I don't mind losing my sovereign. I had a darned good run for my money." The bookie winked at his clerk, and said, "He would have had a bigger run for his money if his horse had won."

The same programme was gone through every year with little variation. We all went to the town house for three months during the London season. It was during my fourth season when we were in London that a great friend of the Bos died in Cornwall. He went to the funeral, taking his valet. When visiting, or travelling, he always took a leather case containing two quart bottles, one to hold brandy, the other whiskey, as he did not like other whiskey than his own. On his return to the London house, he immediately rung his study bell. He told me to bring up his spirit case. He opened it, and said, "I thought so." The bottles were empty. I did not understand what he meant untill he told me the valet was drunk on his way up to town. He said when he put the rug over his knees in the railway carriage he fell down on to him. There had been no time to speak to the valet, or perhaps I could have made things right for him. However, he got the sack.

I was as sorry as though it had been my own brother, for he was a real good fellow-servant. In fact we were like brothers: no need to be cautious as to letting him see or hear anything, as I was sure it would go no farther. We did not have a cross word all the time he was with us. He was so full of fun. He was very fond of rattling two of the copper pot lids together, like cymbals, when I was driving the pony back from the shooting lunches, trying to make it bolt, when it took me all my time to hold the pony in. He would simply laugh at me. Oh, yes, we had some jolly times together. He left, and was replaced by another: where they found him I don't know. A man as different as chalk and cheese in comparison to the other: a creeping, cringing, mischief-making fellow. One could soon tell he had not seen good service. A "mongrel" I called him. We had to be very careful not to let him see or hear anything we did not wish to go farther. He put me in mind of a fellow behind a draper's counter who measures out yards of elastic.

As there were no sons or daughters to "get off," our stay in London was comparatively quiet, except for an occasional big dinner party. At the country house I had thirty-two clocks to wind every week, and the Bos was very particular about their striking at the same time. I don't know if he caught a chill when going to his friend's funeral, or what it was, but he was taken ill shortly after our arrival in the country. He took to his bed and died in three weeks.

Here was a pretty state of affairs. He had no direct heir, so the whole estate went to a distant relation, who was comparatively poor. His wife had to turn out, all servants were discharged. As the town house was the wife's personal property she went there to live, taking the Mongrel to be her butler, as she said the establishment she would keep up would not be large enough for me. The Mongrel had worked himself in there right enough. But I hope I may be saved from such another experience as that funeral. The house was full of relations and friends. The number of wreaths was enormous. The corpse was taken to the Chapel, about a hundred yards from the house. Four of the gentleman visitors took turn in watching, day and night, so that the house was open day and night. A tremendous crowd came on the day of the funeral, for the Bos was well liked and respected by all who knew him, for miles round. A perfect English country gentleman. The Mongrel went about with a white handkerchief to his nose and eyes, especially when the gentry were about. The stupid ass had not known the Bos a month. He behaved as though he had been with him all his life. The two rows of seats for the servants, holding twenty-five, were full, except one vacant seat at the lower end. I, of course, had the seat at the top next the aisle. The Mongrel, of course, came in late to produce effect. He came to the top of our seat. I saw him, and thinking he wanted to squeeze his way down to the vacant seat I politely stepped out into the aisle, to make it easier for him, when he immediately sat down in my seat, fell on his knees, put his face in his handkerchief, and wept copiously. I was left standing in the aisle.

Had it occurred in any other place than a church (a music-hall, for instance) and he had served me the dirty trick I should have caught him by the scruff of the neck, and hauled him out of it. But I did not wish to create any disturbance in such a place and at such a time. The incident did not escape the notice of the widow, who sent the verger, who took me to a seat beside her, in her own pew. Would not the Mongrel have "fancied his chance" had it been him instead of me? He would have thought he was "absolutely It." I quote this instance among many of his tricks, to show what an arrant ass he was. In gentleman's service it must be all "give and take" if servants are to live in peace with one another, but he was

all take and no give, cunning and selfish to the
very core. I never knew what became of him,
and I am sure I don't care. It is curious how
quickly people know if they like each other, even
sometimes only through reading about them. But
in a gentleman's house one has to go on living with
them: whether one likes them or not, one cannot
avoid them like the "man in the street."

.   .   .   .

So this was the end of the best employer (I
hate the word "Master") I ever had.

Gentry, when they are ill, or fancy they are,
have nothing else to do but to go to bed, get in
the best doctors, get the best drugs, and get well,
also can have the best nourishing food that the
earth produces. Not so the poor labourer.

But it is all the same for both rich and poor in
the end. When the old fellow with the scythe and
hour glass comes along it is no use saying, "Wait
a minute." They have both got to go, and the old
world jogs along in the same old way. "Might is
right," and always will be as long as the world
lasts. No time, then, for wishing to undo things
you wish you had not done; no time for doing
things you wish you had done. Too late! You
must wait till the final sorting out, your good deeds
from the bad, and may the good deeds out-balance
the bad deeds, and the opportunities of doing good

that you, through pride, have missed doing. We
shall all stand on the same footing then, receive the
same consideration, and get your deserts. For we
were all born without a shirt. We brought nothing into the world, and we shall take nothing out
of it. In a week or two the widow had collected
her personal belongings, and departed to a smaller
house in Kensington, taking the Mongrel with her,
as butler. I remained on to show the new heir and
his wife where to find things. They brought two
boys who they called footmen with them. Boys
they had taken out of some "Home." The heir
soon got to work and sold a lot of things, horses
and carriages, also hundreds of dozens of wine of
all sorts. He took the keys of the cellars, and was
always present when the packing was going on,
took a list, and locked the door, and took the
keys with him. A very mistrustful sort of man.
He said to me: "I suppose if you wanted to give
notice to leave any situation, you would choose
the month of February, as there are only twenty-
eight days in it." I replied that my days were
not so valuable that I should give such a thing a
single thought. He wanted me to remain on as
his butler, but I declined with thanks.

During the following London season I happened to be passing their town house, where they
were holding a reception. I smiled when I saw

the two footmen, one on each side of the door, they were five feet two, or three, inches tall.   The lady had got the family dress liveries cut down to something like a "fit."   They looked like two ornaments that had fallen off a Christmas cake.

CHAPTER XI

PICTURE to yourself a large room, furnished in the best style that money can buy, couches and easy chairs that one sinks well down among the cushions. On the wide open hearth burns a bright blazing fire of large logs of wood on fire dogs. The lamps shaded so that the light is neither too bright or too dull to read by if so inclined. On the right stands a table on which is whisky, brandy, soda water, and other drinks, and plenty of glasses. On the left stands a table, on which is cigars and cigarettes of the choicest brands. If, after a good day's hunting or shooting, a cup of tea, a hot bath, and a change of clothes, you know of a better " 'Ole" to go to for a couple of hours, till the gong goes, telling you it is time to dress for dinner, well, if you know of a better " 'Ole" go to it.

It was after a good day's hunting, that eight or ten gentlemen were lounging, in what they thought was the easiest positions to crouch among the cushions, each feeling a sort of tired, restful sensation, and feeling on good terms with all the world, in a room as described above, relating some queer incidents and tales appertaining to the world of sport. A whiskey and soda within reach, and a cigar or cigarette between their lips. It was here that I heard the following story told by a Prince of the Blood Royal. I think I had better give it in his own words:—

"I was staying on a visit to my friend, the Duke of Northland, in Ireland, for shooting and hunting, when, after returning from hunting, I changed and went down to the smoking room. I was just about to make myself comfortable when I suddenly thought of an important letter that I should have answered that day, so I went to one of the writing tables to do so.

"On completing it, I rang the bell. Jerkins, the butler, came. I asked him, 'Has the postbag gone yet, Jerkins?' 'I am sorry it has, Your Highness, but I will send a boy with them on a bicycle to the Post Office.' 'Oh, please don't trouble, give me my coat, I will stroll down with the letters myself. There is plenty of time before it is time to dress for dinner.'

"It was a fine night, though dark, and the wind was a bit boisterous. The villiage was a typical Irish one. The only street was unlighted, except by a few parafin lamps in the windows of a shop or two, which simply made darkness visible.

"The Post Office was a sort of general store, where one could buy anything, from a halfpenny candle to a glass of whisky, or a bottle of porter. It was about a mile to the Post Office from the house. As I strolled along the wind seemed to be getting up and more boisterous.

('Hand me the matches, Claud, please; my cigar has gone out while I have been talking. Thanks.') I was just about to turn into the street, when a fellow came running round the corner, with his head down against the wind. His head met me full butt in my 'breadbasket.' I said, 'What the blazes—' but before I could say any more, the fellow had gone runing up the road I had just walked down. I thought no more of it till I got to the Post Office window, when I thought I would look at my watch to see if I was in time for the post, by the light of of the parafin lamp. I put my hand where the watch ought to be, but there was no watch there. I thought, 'So that was why the fellow ran into me rounding the corner. He must have taken my watch.' However, he could not have got far, so I set off after him at my best pace. No wonder the fellow ran off in such a hurry, without speaking. I could distinguish footsteps up the road in front, so hurried on and came up to him. You know at College I could use the gloves a bit, so I at once set about him. I said, 'I'll teach you to steal my watch.' I knocked him down and held on to him in the dark. I took the watch out of his pocket and, giving him a parting punch, I put the watch in my pocket. I hurried back to the house, as I thought it must be getting on for 'dressing time.' Thinking what a fine adventure I should have to relate to the company at dinner, much to the amusement of the ladies. As Jerkins let me in the front door, he told me everyone had gone to dress for dinner, so I went straight up to my room. On turning on the light I went across to the dressing table.

There, in front of me, lay my own watch, where I had left it when changing after coming in from hunting. So I was a watch to the good."

.   .   .   .

We used to visit the above house when it was in its best days, and in full swing. In the servants' hall were two ushers. All one had to do was to go and sit down. They would ask if you would have tea or coffee, and what meat you would like. No trouble in asking people to pass this or that: it was all brought to you. Now that is all over, unless it is in the one or two first-class places that are left. No rules, as of old, are kept. The servants all talk at dinner, mostly of what they like and what they don't like, or about dress, and when the butler is serving out the dinner they say, "Oh, give me a piece off there" or "I'll have that piece there." This is the sort of talk that goes on: "When I'm married I shall not do any of the washing. Nor shall I get up in the morning to get my husband's breakfast. He will have to bring my breakfast up to me in bed. I shall have a bicycle, and go to the pictures every day, and to dances at night." A nice sort of helpmate for a working man! If the butler don't "hold the candle" to the lot of them, and try to please them, they will soon find means to oust him out of his job, by fair means or foul. Sometimes they say, "Oh, our last butler used to give us a drop of some-

thing short before we went to bed." So if the
present one does not (even though he pays for it
out of his own pocket) to keep on the right side
of them, they will find means to proceed as above.
A very few upper servants hold their places by
their own merit, but by what the other servants
choose to say about them. Neither does a butler
get a good place on his merits. If he happens to
be known to some of the upper servants in the
place, he will get the position right enough, in preference to all others, in spite of his disabilities, if
he uses enough palm oil. What a wonderful thing
palm oil is! If you want rooms or a house, you
have to use it, and the one who uses most gets the
house or rooms. If you want to bring out an inven-
tion unlimited palm oil must be used, or the in-
vention sticks where it is. If a registry office
knows of a really good situation going it does not
go to the first suitable man who applies to them
for it. Oh, no, it goes to the man who produces
most palm oil. Independent of this their charges
are generally sixpence in the pound on wages to be
received. Thus, if a man is to get eighty pounds
a year the registry office gets two pounds, and the
employer pays them as much or more. If that is
not buying and selling human beings for work, I
should like to know what is. Registry offices will
often put in an advertisement in the *Morning
Post*, requiring a servant for a good post, good

wages, in fact make it look as tempting as possible. On a servant applying to them for the place they say, "Oh, that place has just been taken, but we are sure to have just such another in a day or so, if you will put your name on our books; our booking fee is half-a-crown." Now, supposing forty servants from all parts of the country either by letter or personally apply and pay their booking fee, there is a clear profit of five pounds, less the cost of four shillings for the advertisement. Not at all a bad business proposition. Possibly they will give or post one a list of places, some of which one has allready refused without their help. The others will probably be filled. A servant can easily wear out several pairs of boots, wasting time and money, runing after these will o' the wisps."

The registry offices are very persistant in their endeavours to collect these booking fees, though nothing was said about booking fees in the alluring advertisement. A bill for half-a-crown is posted to each client. Even if they still persist and spend as much as two shillings in postage they are still in pocket, that is if they eventually get the half-crown. I have had this experience, but I replied, "I herewith return you your account re booking fee, as I am not paying money away to-day for nothing. When you get me a situation I will pay your charges."

Every endeavour is being made by printing

articles in the newspapers to persuade girls to go
into service: even so far as to point out the advan-
tages of such a training would be to them when
they marry and have a home of their own.   They
may be able to find a man, though now at the present time there is not enough men to go round.
But having found the man, where are they going
to find a home, or even rooms?   Of course they
must work or starve, but is there any reason why
a girl should give up her liberty in order to live?
I once heard an old butler say, "If I had a dozen
daughters not one of them should go into gentleman's service."

I noticed in the paper the other day that an institution was started to train seven thousand girls
to be servants: but they won't do it.   They may
turn out seven thousand makeshifts, they may
learn them the mechanical side of the work, to
clean a room, make a bed, wash out a few "smalls,"
clean silver, or a grate, make a cake, but they
won't make a servant.   The first thing they will
have to do is to break their will, for no servant may
have a will of their own.   She must learn to take a
torrent of ill temper and abuse, and look as though
she likes it that way, but on no account can she, or
he, have a temper of their own.   Often, when
things have gone wrong between Master and Mistress, the servants are used as a safety valve.
They "let out" at them right and left, nothing is

right, all wrong, the servant dare not answer, or
out you go, and when your character is applied for
in your next place, "Bad tempered and insolent"
is the verdict. The poor servant can try for a
place till she is tired, but she won't get one. She
must then either get married or go on the streets.
A great deal will have to be taken on trust, as to
"character" of this flood of girls that are being
"trained" in masses. Servants, like birds, must be
caught when young. The girls of the present,
having had a few years of liberty, if put into service, would be constantly beating their wings
against the bars of their cage, so to speak, and
would never settle down to it for long together.
Their dominant thought would always be, "When
is it my turn to go out?" And having got out,
are worrying themselves about the time they have
to get back. What they will miss most is their
freedom on Sundays. Which reminds me of the
following chorus to an old song, sung by a modern
"slavey."

> "Six days a week with all my might,
> I keep the pots and kettles bright,
> And keep the cobwebs out of sight;
> But I must go out on Sunday."

It is not often servants get any thrills during
their life in service, except a burglary, or the
house catches alight. But a thrill of a different

sort occurred in a house in the country some time ago. The household had assembled one morning for family prayers, all were present except the ladies-maid. The Bos had two gentleman "friends" who had called to see him that morning, and they consented to join in the family supplications. Each of them sat near the door. The Bos enquired where Miss Hadum was? One of the servants replied that she was not attending prayers that morning, as she had a headache, and asked to be excused. The Bos sent a servant to fetch her, saying he would not begin prayers till she came. Eventually the ladies-maid came and took her place. At the conclusion of prayers, the servants all went out in single file. As the ladies-maid was about to go out of the door a hand was placed on each of her shoulders. "She" proved to be a man convict who had escaped from a prison some miles away, a year before. One occasionally meets a man who has effamite manners and looks, even to the voice. It only requires the clothes to complete the delusion.

A similar case occurred in Grosvenor Place, London, about thirty years ago. This man acted as young ladies-maid. But I should fancy the ladies were inclined to kick themselves after the deception was discovered. Perhaps they felt like the old fellow who had wound up his clock every night before going to bed, for fifty years, and then

discovered it was an eight-day clock, and only required winding once a week.   Or something like
the gardener felt who used to court the cook.   He
was not allowed in the house, but used to go behind
the laurels under the larder window, and give a
peculiar whistle.   The cook knew the signal.   So
they used to have a game at "Romeo and Juliet."
But the Missus had noticed the whistle often.
She was determined to find out what it meant, so
went to the larder, and sent the cook away.   The
gardener could not distinguish her, as the window
was covered with wire gauze.   The first thing he
asked was, "Where's the old gal?"   Then there
was another gardener's post vacant.

I believe his Satanic Majesty plays tricks on us
human beings sometimes.   He certainly did on
me on an occasion of a large house party for the
Ascot Races, in the year that Clorane won the
Hunt Cup.

Several other valets, who I had met at their own
and other places were there, and a corresponding
number of ladies-maids.   The house had been
taken for the race week.   I also knew the butler
previously.   On the Hunt Cup day the valets had
hired a waggonette to take us up to the course,
each of us paying our part of the cost.   We dare
not start till the gentry had driven away from the
front door, in case we were wanted at the last
minute.   My Bos was a bit fidgetty and peppery.

A few minutes before it was time to start the butler came into the pantry and said he had lost a five pound note.   He was a man who got excited when in a tight corner—what is called "flustered." This incident was unplesant, as it put us all, more or less, under a certain amount of suspicion.   He said: "I had it here a short time ago."   He searched his pockets again, but the note was not to be found.   We all set to work to look for it.   I noticed when he came into the pantry he was screwing some waste paper up in his hand, which he threw into the empty fire-grate.   We searched this, but there was no five pound note there.   In the meantime the butler had to go to the front door to "see them off."   The valets then said, "Come on, we need not wait any longer," and away they went to the side door, and mounted the waggon-ette.   I waited in the pantry, as I dare not go till the gentry had gone; besides, I did not like the idea of the five pound note being lost.

Under most pantry washing up sinks a pail is kept to receive the scrapings of breakfast and desert plates, also for emptying the tea leaves out of the tea pots.

I stood there alone wondering, when the thought struck me to look into this pail, which was nearly full of rubbish.   At first I could see nothing but tea leaves, and pieces of paper, but on turning these over I discovered the five pound note.   It

was all wet and stained by the tea leaves. "Now,
Mr Butler," thinks I, "I have a surprise for you."
At this juncture great shoutings came from the
side door, "Come on, Nabob" (that's what they
used to call me) "We are off, not going to wait
any longer for you. We shall miss the first race."
I heard the waggonette drive off. I was in a bit
of a dialemma. I wanted to be off. The butler
had not returned. I did not like to leave the note
on the table, with no one about, in case it got stolen
in reality. So I dried the note with a cloth, put
it in my pocket, and decided to give it to him on
my return from the races. I darted off after the
waggonette, and caught them up as they were going out at the lodge gates. I never had much
money for betting, as I had to consider those at
home, and send most of my wages there. But
something within me told me that Clorane would
win the race, that I was almost tempted to put
more on it than I could afford, but I only had five
shillings "each way," and Clorane won at ten to
one. It is said that fortune knocks at every man's
door once. I suppose that was my chance, for I
have never seen anything before, or since, sticking
out like Clorane, but I had not the money to in-
vest. Even if I had to any great amount, perhaps
ten pounds, the probability is that the bookie
would have "hopped it," rather than pay out a
hundred and ten pounds, as I did not go into any

ring to bet. However, I ended up by being two
pounds to the good on the day's racing. On our
arrival back at the house, I thought how pleased
the butler would be. I handed him the note, which
had got dry in my pocket. He immediately flew
into a terrible temper, said I had stolen the note
in the morning, had taken it, and used it on the
course, that I had won money with it, and if I had
lost instead of wining I should have kept it quiet
and said nothing. I tried to explain the circumstances in which I found it, pointed out the stains
of the tea leaves on the note, and why I had left
in the morning without giving it to him, but all to
no purpose. Everyone believed as he did. I was
well derided in front of everybody at supper that
night, and jeered at. It nearly led to a fight, but
I managed to restrain myself. I was cut out of
their circle of friendship, and no doubt looked
upon with suspicion to this day. I, on the contrary, thought how thankful everyone should have
been, for if the note had been thrown away with
the rubbish every servant in the house would always been under suspicion. I argued, supposing
I had used and changed the note, what were the
odds that I should have the same note, stained with
tea leaves, handed back to me on the racecourse?
But as I was alone and had no witnesses when I
found the note in the pail, my statement was not
believed. If this was not a trick of the devil, I

don't know what is. I thereupon made a vow
(which I have not kept) that should I ever find
anything else of value I would keep it dark and
say nothing.   If ever I see servants leaving their
money or jewellery about I tell them it is not fair
to the other servants, for should it be lost, or stolen,
every servant in the house is suspected, and under
suspicion.

A case of this sort occurred in my younger days,
when I was under butler. The footmen had
missed money out of a drawer in their bedroom.
A char-woman came in from the villiage once a
week to scrub out the men servants' bedrooms.
The butler and the clerk of the works marked some
coins, and put them in the drawer. The char-
woman did not come into the servants' hall to dinner. After dinner the footmen went to their
rooms, and found some money missing. The
woman was called to the butler's room, and
searched; she had the money, and confessed she
was the culprit.

.   .   .   .

After a brief stay at home with my wife and
son, my late employer being dead, and my purse
not being a very long one, it behoved me to find
another situation.   In this I had no difficulty, as
my references were of the best.   Perhaps it would
have been better for me through life had I taken
smaller places, but my aim was always upward and

onward, though I could never hope to attain the very top of the tree, being three inches short of six feet.   I was still full of energy, and could never bear to be idle.   I could not stand or sit about and do nothing but talk: my aim was to "Do."   In my spare time I would do photographing, music practice on my violin, needlework or woolwork.   It is curious what a "funny fish" a man developes into who is shut up inside a house all his life.

CHAPTER XII

NOTHING short of being in the service of the family of a Marquess would suit me this time: at a large Castle not many miles from the South Coast. The Marquess was seldom in residence, he preferring either his London, or one of his other country houses to live in. There was a family of four or five sons, all over six feet high, and two twin daughters. I have taken a note in for one of the ladies, but the fact of their being exactly alike, and they used to dress alike, that I did not know which of them to hand it to. They would ask me, "Who's it for?" I said, "It's for Lady Jane." "Then it's for me," she replied. They were all Aristocrats of the first water, though there seemed to be a "kink" in the brain of some of them, for they did some curious things at times.

There was a large lake in the park, full of fish. At certain periods nothing pleased the Marquis better than to get a lot of men off the estate, and with a net reaching across the lake, drag it from one end to the other. Some of the men had to walk in the water to support the net. On the bank a fire was lit, and a large kettle, supported gypsy fashion, full of hot gin and beer, mixed. With

this he would supply the men pretty frequently,
till they got merry. It pleased him to see the
men topple over in the water. It was quite a day
of amusement and fun. The Marquess would
stand on the bank and shout at the men: "Now
Edwards, you are doing nothing." Edwards replied, "Beg pardon, my Lord, I'm working like a
b—— horse."

When in residence he would have his own butler
(who had been in his service for thirty years—he
had pensioned him off) up from the village. On
these occasions I had to take a step down, and
act as groom of the chambers. On one occasion
the Marquess sent him a telegram from London
saying, "Twenty to dinner." This made every
one busy, but we were ready. When the Marquess arrived in the evening his butler said:
"None of the company has arrived yet, my Lord."
The Marquess replied: "You old fool, don't you
know what day it is?" It was the first of April.
When he was packing up to go anywhere, and
when his valet was packing, he would pitch the
things at him. Hair brushes, boots, anything,
saying, "Take that, and that." The valet had to
be quick to dodge them. When his valet put his
account book for wages and other items on his
writing table for payment he always found it
thrown under the table; he would put it on the
table again, but found it under the table again.

So it would go on, till it pleased him to pay it. But one could not help liking them all, for they were Aristocrats of the first water. The son, who was always in residence, and ran the show, was also the Master of hounds—their own pack.

On the occasion of a large dinner party the old butler, who was an enormous big man, and had very large feet, took an empty toast rack off the table in front of the Marquess, to whom he was very attentive, dropped it on the floor, went to pick it up, kicked it, sent it skidding along the polished floor, right under a table in the corner of the room. One of the servants said quietly, "Goal."

To anyone outside the Castle on a certain early morning in November, it would seem evident that something out of the common run of things were going on inside, for lights were flitting here and there; every servant was about and doing earlier than usual. In fact it was the opening Meet of the season.

> "Wee'l join the glad throng, and go trotting along,
> For wee'l all go a-hunting to-day."

And great throngs were expected that morning. Preparations had to be made accordingly, and as the Marquess was not in residence, I had to take command, and see that everything was in order. A hunt breakfast had to be prepared for fifty, or more if required, in the Baronial Hall: a fine appartment with suits of armour standing at intervals round the walls. Old regimental flags, dating back to the Wars of the Roses, and Cromwell's time, hung from the walls higher up. A fine roof with carved oak rafters. At nine o'clock people could be seen wending their way from all directions through the Park towards the Castle. Men on foot from miles around, intending to have a "run for it." Later on ladies and farmers' wives and daughters came in dogcarts, governess cars, and carriages of various sorts, in many of which were children, delighted to see the hounds. I am writing of the time before that "stink pot," the motor car, was invented, which rush backwards and forwards across the line the fox would take, cutting him off here, cutting him off there, so that the poor devil don't know "where he are." It was not a large meet like one sees at Manby Gate, but it was a fine company. Farmers, well-to-do tradesmen, who had left their horses at the stables, came trooping towards the front entrance of the Castle. It is astonishing what a sence of shyness farmers, and such like, show when asked to sit down at the table of their "betters," but this wears off after a bit after a glass or two of old ale, or a whiskey and soda. It was always the custom of having an enormous round of cold spiced beef, at one end of the table, and which was well patron-

ized. It took two men to carry it in, one at each
end of the great silver dish. Besides this were
game pies, pork pies, legs of roast pork, cold hams,
pastry, apple tarts and cream, jellies, cakes.
Cheese and butter all down the table. At every
space between were jugs of home brewed ale,
sherry, claret, port and whiskey. Also choice
flowers from the greenhouses.

Now the crowd is getting greater outside. The
ladies are shown into the library, where trays of
refreshments are laid out. Something light, cherry
brandy, sloe gin, coffee, cakes and biscuits. In
the meantime footmen are running about among
the carriages, and gentry who will not dismount
and come into the Castle, with trays of cherry
brandy, sloe gin, whiskey and soda, cake and
biscuits, perswading them to partake of it, as the
morning is chilly, though fine. The ladies say,
"No thanks," but after second thoughts, "I will,
just a thimbleful of cherry brandy." She cocks
her little finger, makes a face as though she don't
like it. But she does all the time. The foot runners, who did not care to enter into the Baronial
Hall, were well provided with ale and bread and
cheese in the courtyard. Neither was the huntsman and whips forgotten, though they at first refused, but were persuaded to take a little "jumping powder" in a shamefaced sort of way, as much
as to say, "you made me take it, though I didn't

want to do it." "Ah, ah, good morning, my
Lady," says old General Currypepper, raising his
hat, "What a lovely morning." "Yes," replied
my Lady, "I think the scent will lie, and we shall
have a good run." "Won't you go in and have
something?" This to Lord Foozler, with a window in his eye. "No; thanks awfully, my Lady.
It is much too early in the day for me." "Ah,
who is this coming up the drive curvetting sideways on his nag like a crab?" "Why, it's Gusset,
the tailor. He rides as though he sat on a box of
tin tacks." "But, who is that on the outskirts of
the crowd?" "Why! No one else but our friend,
the Curate; on old Ribbones, an old hurdle
jumper, he has borrowed from the baker. Ribbones is cocking his ears, and dancing as if in expectation of a great treat." The sight of the
hounds and scarlet coats seemed to have taken ten
years off the age of Ribbones. The young Curate
was an exception as Curates go. Well built, and
athletic, light curly hair, laughing blue eyes. He
was not the sort to be found drinking tea in old
ladies' drawing rooms. He did not think it necessary, because one happened to be religious, to go
about with a long face, and a miserable look. His
idea was, "O, be joyful in the Lord." He was a
favourite with all who knew him; being of a good
family. There was not an atom of "Swank" about
him. He had not been at his post long before he

had got enough money together to build a tin gym-
nasium and reading room, and he kept the young
men and youths together by his lectures, readings,
and boxing lessons (for he was a good boxer).
He would teach them that religion was shown
by our daily actions, and if they were slow to understand it he punched it into them, and was
always pleased if any among them were good
enough with the gloves to give him a "licking."
In his sermons he was outspoken, although the
gentry were among the congregation. He often
came very near hitting the nail bang on the head
when he spoke of lying, backbiting, slandering,
and bad tempers. If the cap fitted, any of them
were welcome to wear it. I remember him finish-
ing his sermon by reminding them that there was
no room in Heaven for people with bad tempers.

In the Baronial Hall things were going on mer-
rily. After the first glass or two, they let their
tongues loose, conversation became general. All
the visiting valets were enlisted to assist as waiters
for the occasion. "Say, waiter," said a farmer,
with his mouth full of cold beef, "What's that
purty wobbly stuff over there?" "Blanc-mange,"
said the waiter. "Right ho! Gie me some Blue-
monge." By the time we had got to handing them
little glasses of sloe gin, cherry brandy, cigars and
cigarettes, one of them, thinking it was only a
sample of cherry brandy, said, "Hi, waiter; I likes

this stuff fine. Bring I some in a joog." On one of the young Lords looking in, he noticed a farmer drinking claret, so had a glass himself, observing, "A decent drop of claret that, Huskley!" "Aye, my Lord, it be purty, but I have been drinking it for the past half hour but I don't seem to get any 'forrader.'" Many were the jokes bandied across the table after they had got more at home with each other. Those that were wise got up and went towards the stables where their horses were. On the appearance of the "Master," everyone seemed to have a touch of the "fidgetts." The carriages and dogcarts began to draw off to a point of vantage where a good view of the expected run could be obtained. Suddenly a few blasts of the Master's horn is heard, and cries of, "They're off," a general scuttle off to the stables. Those of the foot runners who know the country are taking short cuts across the park and fields, towards the covert appointed to be drawn first. The hounds are waved in by huntsman and whips. Everyone is on the tapis of expectation. The huntsman shouting at a hound by name occasionally. After a time comes the "View Hollo," for they have found "Reynard" at home. He slips away out of the far end of the covert, taking a line across country. A few blasts on the horn, "Toodly toot, toodly toot," and away they go. Our friend the Curate has trotted Ribbones to see the throw off, just that and nothing more. But Ribbones has ideas of his own. With ears pricked, away he bolts after the rest of the field, and clears his jumps like an old hand. The pace became hot, soon stragglers were left behind, foot runners were taking what they thought a short cut across country to the spot they thought the fox was making for. The line was lenthening out, a few croppers could be seen, but Ribbones kept his feet. After fifty minutes clinking run the hounds pulled down their fox. But who is that close up to the hounds, in the black coat? Why, it's the Curate! Ribbones may have taken him against his will. Who knows? But what will his Bishop have to say about it. We all forgave him, though he does button his collar at the back of his neck.

But let us get back to the Banqueting Hall. Fox hunting never interested me a great deal, except the cleaning of scarlet coats, leather breeches, and top boots, which I could do as well as any man. When the hounds left the Castle, all the waiters left too. They wanted to see the draw, so that only I and the footmen were left to clear up and relay the table, in case any of the hunting folk came back that way. We left it ready untill four o'clock, as it was open house that day. The first footman was nearly as old as myself. I often wondered why he had not got farther advanced, but I soon found out. I asked them all to let the drink

alone till after hounds had gone, when I would give
them one, as I could not be everywhere at once,
and there was plenty of drinks of all sorts about.
When we were clearing away, the first footman
brought a butler's trayfull of dirty glasses to the
pantry, dropped the lot flat on to the floor, said
he thought the tray was on the table. I could then
see what was the matter with him, he could scarcely
stand he was so drunk. I made him drink a pint
of hot mustard and water, and after he had
brought the drink up, put him to bed, as he was
no use to me. Some servants are all right as long
as they keep away from the drink, but the first
chance they see, especially of getting it for nothing, they cannot resist getting drunk. When I
did leave, they made him butler, but a few months
after, one fine morning, they found him drowned
in the lake! Being younger then I am now, I did
not like the idea of taking the step down to groom
of the chambers when the old and confidential butler came up to take command. So I thought I
could be doing better. I told his Lordship I did
not like playing second fiddle on these occasions.
"Second fiddle," he replied. "You ought to think
yourself lucky to be in the band at all." Although
this was not a bad sort of place, there were no old
usages, no "Sprit de Corps," among the servants,
which was fast dying out. There was no pride in
wearing the liveries of this or that high family as

in the old days. Things were detoriating into a
mere scrabble, and less and less servants were kept.
I don't suppose there are a dozen grooms of the
chambers in Great Britain at the present day.
Some there are who have to do those duties and
valet combined. When in such a case they have
their hands full.

A rather unusual thing happened at a house in
Bucks that I was staying at. The foxhounds met
there that day on the lawn opposite the front door.
The hunt breakfast was ready, when suddenly the
whole pack of hounds rushed into the dining room.
I suppose they could smell the food, and, as
hounds are never fed on hunting days, nothing
since the night previous, untill they get back to
the kennels after hunting, they were hungry. In
a few minutes everything had disappeared. Beef,
chicken, hams, pies, bread, pastry, all had been
eaten. Dishes, plates, glasses, knives and forks,
decanters of wine and spirits were all over the floor
and broken. The huntsman could not get into
the room, so the whips broke the glass and opened
the French windows, and they drove them out that
way. It spoilt that day's hunting, for hounds
won't hunt when full of food.

"Jacko" was the name of a monkey we had
there. A sea captain had sent it as a present to
his Lordship. When he arrived, in a tea chest,
I had to unpack him. I wondered if he would

fly out at me when I took the top boards off. But
I found he was only a black baby monkey, and
very affectionate, and very mischevious. We put
him in a loose horse box, the last one of a long
row, with thatched roofs. Sometimes he would
get loose, climb up the water pipes at the side of
the house, into the bedrooms. He was fond of
anything shiny and bright, so he took the jewellery
down to his box. He was very fond of a black
kitten, which would sleep between his legs. He
would turn her fur over with his fingers, as though
he was looking for fleas. The stablemen found
him handy for pulling out the weeds between the
cobble stones in the stable yard, but if they did
not watch when he had pulled them all up, and
chain him in another place, he would pull the
stones up as well. He grew very fast, and shed
his first teeth just like a human baby. When the
stablemen went for their beer at eleven o'clock
each morning to the village pub, Jacko went too,
and had a drink of it. One day he got his chain
off the bar, and went off down the road jumping
from one tree to another, with all the stablemen
after him. He went thus for half a mile, when
the crossbar of his chain got between the fork of
a branch. One of them got up the tree, caught
him, and led him home. He grew to be over three
feet high when standing, but he got so mischevious
and did so much damage that his Lordship pre-

sented him to the Zoo. When they put him in the cage with the other monkeys, he was soon Bos of the show. He would catch the other monkeys by the tail and swing them round and round. So they had to give him a cage to himself. His Lordship also had the best bulldog that I ever saw. If we told him to seize a chair leg, or a table, he would never leave go, until we twisted his tail. Near his kennel was a meadow in which the donkey used to graze. The donkey could get close to his kennel. What they said to each other no one knows. But one day the dog slipped his collar, went straight for the donkey, seized it by the throat, and hung on, untill someone went and screwed his tail, till he let go.

We had one other curosity at this place, in the shape of an old fat German cook. She would not give the servants enough food. I could not speak German, but I told her in pretty plain English that we should look after ourselves out of the dining room food, not to take it after it came out of the dining room, but before it went in. I fancy I can see her now. She wore elastic side boots, and the fat of her legs used to protude and hang over the tops of her boots.

The footman at this place was a lively sort of fellow, very smart and clean in dress and person. He had a habit of sitting and swinging on top of a sort of nursery, brass-topped fireguard in the pan-

try.   One day he swang it out too far, went backwards, his head under the grate.   In falling, he
brought down the kettle of water, the kettle landing on his shirt front.   Fortunately the water was
not boiling.   I laughed so loud that the Bos came
out to see what was the matter.   The Bos was a
sort of "I-will-be-obeyed" sort of man.

On one occasion he hired four men to clear some
land to enlarge the kitchen garden.   It being in
winter the weather was terribly cold and wet.
They took their dinners, cold meat and bread, into
the stokehole by the greenhouses, and to heat their
tea bottles.   The Bos came along, and turned
them all out, saying he was not going to allow them
to warm themselves by his fire.   One day he had a
letter for post after the postman had gone.   He
rushed out of the front door and shouted, as he
could see him down the carriage drive; so the postman turned back to see what he wanted.   He said,
"Why don't you run, fellow, when I call you?"
"Because the Government pays me to walk!" replied the postman.   Query: Did anyone ever see
a postman run?

It was at this place that the Bos asked me where
I kept his cartridges.   I replied, "In my bedroom."   "Oh," he said, "It's much too damp for
cartridges in there."   But it was not too damp for
the butler to sleep in.   One day during a sharp
summer thunderstorm two men had taken shelter

under the trees just inside the lodge gates, which
led out on to the high road.   The Bos spied them
from a distance, called his gardener, put on his
mackintosh, went down to them and said: "What
are you doing on my property?"   "Only taking
shelter from the storm, mister."   "Well get out of
it, you're trespassing."   "Where can we get shelter," they asked.   "I don't know, and don't care.
Get out."   So they put up their coat collars and
went outside the gates, then turned back and
shouted, after putting their hands to their mouths,
and making a noise like a young motor horn:
"Say, guv'nor, you don't happen to be a bookmaker, do you?"   That's the sort of treatment
they got, after four years' fighting in France, in
order that he, and more like him, could live in
safety and comfort.

Footmen generally have to sleep in let-down
beds in the servants' hall, which, outside of being
unhealthy, is not nice for the servants when they
assemble for breakfast.   Perhaps the footman had
been out with the carriage to a ball the night before; all the same he has to turn out the same as
usual in order that the other servants may have
their breakfasts.   A butler's bedroom is generally
close to the area door, damp and unsanitry, and
would be condemned as a sleeping place in any
other house but the gentry's.   Generally in the
room is a cistern that is constantly trickling water,

and a soil pipe from above close to his pillow, with periodical rushes down the pipe.   I once knew of a hall boy who had to sleep in a let-down bed in the passage leading from the area door.   Of course he could not go to bed untill everyone else had gone: but anything is good enough for men servants.

CHAPTER XIII

THE six years I was in service of a Russian Princess is far too great a human tragedy for me to write of in detail. Call her what you will, exile, refugee, she was one of the most considerate, amiable ladies that ever walked this earth, though misfortune after misfortune met her at every turn. Her manner quickly showed that she had been used to moving in Royal Courts. She had two sons and one daughter. In the early days, after they had come over from Russia, they were, without doubt, watched by Russian spies. Whenever the two sons, aged eighteen and twenty-one, went to town, which they did nearly every day, I always had to go with them as a sort of bodyguard. Their mother, the Princess, was afraid they would be spirited away out of her charge, and she not know which way they went. The porters and police got to know them at Victoria Station. As soon as they saw us get out of the train they were tumbling over one another to see who should get us a taxi: they were sure of a tip of a few shillings.

These two sons had a fine talent for engineering. They were among the very first to build an areoplane in this country, at Brooklands, with the help of three mechanics. But, alas, they built it of such enormous size that the engine power they had was not one third powerful enough to make it take the air. Had they built two smaller ones instead they might have made a good start. When the enormous thing was finished a large company of Lords and Ladies came down, broke a bottle of champayne over her nose. We then pushed it out in the open, set the engine going full speed, but the thing would not move. There it stuck till dark, when we pushed it back into the shed. Their energies deserved a better fate.

When first they came to England they kept up a good establishment. But after losing one estate after another in Russia, they had to do with less and less servants. Eventually the eldest son married the daughter of a large store owner in London, but the wife's fortune was so tied up that the husband had no control of it.

Whether it be in palace or castle, cottage or hut, the sudden stoppage of all income is bound to produce some very unplesant happenings and circumstances. The jewels were many and valuable. These were sold to keep things going, but even the proceeds of the sale would not keep things going for long. Servants' wages were periodically becoming due, ard could not be paid. Consequently the footmen were the first to go on strike, then the housemaids, then the kitchen and scullery-maids. They would not go without their wages, but hung about the house without working, nevertheless they had to be fed and lodged. As the days went by the atmosphere became more humid, the servants began to quarrel among themselves; they could not be turned out except by brute force. The chauffeur had a fight with the butler, an ex-Life Guardsman, who stood six feet four in his socks: the chauffeur hit the butler on the head with a stone jug, and broke the jug. Of course the butler could have crushed his neck with one hand had he wished, but as we all knew the chauffeur always carried a revolver in his hip pocket, we rushed between them and got the chauffeur away, for we did not want to see murder done. The secretary went to town to see if he could raise enough money to pay off the servants who were on strike, and let them depart. But if one wants to know the value of money, let him try and borrow some. Eventually they were partly paid, and promiced the remainder later, but which they never got, so they departed. The butler had advanced the Princess certain sums of money which, together with his wages owing, was a considerable amount. He took the whole of the family plate, as security, and then his departure. Thus there were only three servants left. The cook, myself, valet, and an odd man. Want of money and a splash of loyalty, made us stay on. Why is it that a lady with such a kind angelic disposition is made to suffer the torments of the damned? Whereas a bad-tempered, grasping, immoral cat of a woman can have everything she desires, a kind of cat who no servants can live with more than a month.

For years my wages were not fully paid. I had not the heart to leave them, though there were little hopes of better times. In the end I came away with one hundred and seventy pownds owing to me, and it is still owing, with no chance of my ever getting it. For it is no use whipping a dead horse.

I observed the other day that the married son's comings and goings were notified in the fashionable column in the daily papers. Thusly: "The Prince and Princess Wontpopski left their town house in Portman Square for Paris to-day." I knew they were in town, so called on the off-chance of seeing the Prince, but was told by the butler, "Not at home," and he did not know when he would be back. I said I would write. I wrote, but got no reply. I called again. The butler said he had gone to the country, he did not know when he would be back. Now this is a thing "no fellah can understand"—notifying their movements in Society papers, and yet goes about owing his late valet one hundred and seventy pounds wages. What rotten Swank!

At the time of my leaving them my wife was gradually going blind. She eventually went quite blind. All that could be done for her was done. I took her to a Harley Street specialist several times, at a guinea a visit, when he could do nothing more for her. I took her periodically to King's College Hospital. She became an in-patient, remaining there three months. They took both her eyes out. After a time she could distinguish shaddows, but eventually went quite blind again. It was at this stage of affairs, that I thought I would try and get some other employment than gentleman's service, in order that I could at least be home at night, to see to things. Though my wife could find her way about the house by feeling the furniture, there was still the danger of her setting herself alight. Some said: "Why not go as waiter?" Easier said than done, as those who have tried it will tell you. I tried to get temporary work, such as cleaning silver, and other daily work about a house, but could not get enough of it to earn a living. After consultation with my brother, who owned a taxi, he said, "Why not go in for this game? I get a living at it." But before I could do this Scotland Yard has something to say to one about it. Firstly I had to get proof of character from last employer, and two other householders. After this one has to learn one's way, and the nearest way, about eight square miles of streets of

London, must know all the clubs, hotels, railway and tube stations, all the theatres, music halls and cinemas, hospitals, police stations and morturies, cemetries, and prisons, and the nearest way to get to them from any given point.   All the docks and wharves, and principal banks, museums, and principal buildings.   There is a school for learning all this, for which they charge seven pounds for three months' tuition, but one must be very clever, and have an extraordinary good memory to pass the examinations in six months.   When one thinks he knows enough, he goes up to Scotland Yard, only to be floored perhaps by the very first question. They then tell you to come up again in a fortnight. Studying large maps helps one a great deal, but that is not enough.   The police inspectors will ask what colour such a building is somewhere in the East End, whether the road is of wood or asphalt. They can then tell if you have been there, or only learnt by the maps.   The same questions of every part of London.   It has been said that there is more study required to pass this examination than that of taking a degree at Oxford or Cambridge. But I persevered.   Some days I would be absent from the school, and take a tour by 'bus and tram to the East End, as far as Woolwich and Greenwich, and walk back, searching the streets as I came.   By the evening I was as tired as a dog. On other days I would go South, North, or West, exploring and taking notes. But the fact of my not being used to being out of doors in all weathers, in the cold and wet, I was soon knocked up, not getting proper food, and poor food at the best. I soon got pluerisy. I was laid up for three months, the pain was so great that I wished I could die. I got so weak and run down that a swelling came out, similar to a large boil, at the back of my neck. Also I showed an eruption on my side to the doctor. "Why, man," he said, "You have got the shingles!" I, who had never had so much as a pimple on my skin before. "Good Lord," I thought, "is there anything else that goes with driving a taxi?" However, I pulled through, and gradually got stronger. As Spring advanced I wanted to get out of doors, but first I thought I would try getting out of bed, which I did, and fell on the floor: there I remained. I was too weak to get into bed again, so remained there till someone came and lifted me in bed again. So I was not so strong as I thought I was. After another fortnight of bed I asked the doctor if I could go out of doors for a little while, it being a fine sunshiny day. He said I might try. I had been practising walking across the room for some days. I got my clothes on, but as soon as I got out in the fresh air everything went round and round, houses, street and all, and I fell flat on the pavement. They took me back to bed. After a bit I got strong enough to resume my studies. I was determined to master it. I passed the Scotland Yard test in nine months after I began, including the time I was ill. Then came the examination as to knowledge of twenty-five miles round London, but this was not so severe a test as the other. I soon passed. Now came the time to learn to drive a taxi. They will not begin to learn one untill one has passed the knowledge test, as only about ten per cent, got through. Four learners get inside the taxi, one at the wheel, with an instructor sitting beside him. Each one gets forty minutes' drive. As we advance in learning the instructor takes them gradually to the busiest parts of London, putting one in tight corners. I used to like driving in traffic. Sometimes the language was a bit flowery. Such as, "Oh, yes, you'd do to drive a b—— funeral," when looking for a chance to pass something in front in Regent Street or Piccadilly. When I saw a chance I let it go and shot past. "That's it, smash the damned thing up," says the instructor. All the old horse cab drivers got through with a minor examination. All they had to do was to learn to drive a taxi. During the time I was learning I used to go to a man I knew, who had a few cars for private hire. He promiced to learn me a bit about motors. One day I was attempting to start up a large six cylinder car. It was cold and obstinate, but I put all my strength into it: got a backfire. It felt as though my arm had gone over the roofs of the houses. It would have been better if I had broken my arm. I had lacerated my arm and shoulder muscles, and was painful for years: whenever I moved my arm my shoulder went click, clack. In passing the driving test at Scotland Yard one has to back the taxi round a corner, and through a narrow arch-way. The first time I tried I just touched the post with one of the wings. The next time, after being put back a month, I was worse. Yet I could always do it when practicing round a street corner. Then the boys all came back from the war. Thousands of taxis were put on the streets, and the "game was not worth the candle." If I had kept on with it, this history would not have been written, for I should have been dead long ago, for I could not stand the outdoor life in the winter, the cold and the wet. It was like taking a hothouse plant and leaving it outdoors on a frosty night. The spirit was willing but the flesh was weak. I had got thin and ill. So I decided, if I wished to live, I must give up this job, and go back into gentleman's service, for I knew no other trade or profession. I estimate that this taxi venture cost me a hundred pounds as I earned no money while learning. Thus it can be seen, that although a taximan may look greasy and oily, he must have a head with something in it above his shoulders. It was scarcely a fitting occupation for a man who had always been in the politest society, but if my constitution would have stood it, I would have held on, in order to attain my object. However, I suppose there are greater disappointments in life than this. So it was "Nil Desperandum" with me. After explaining my position to my last employer, his Lordship gave me a reference. But just after the war very few people were engaging men servants. On the contrary, they were getting rid of them as fast as they could, and employing parlourmaids in their places, as they were cheaper, and they still continue to employ them in place of men. Consequently there were hundreds of men whose sole experience was gained by valeting an officer, or waiting in the officers' mess. They then called themselves butlers and valets, all wanting situations. Anyhow, I had to get some sort of employment, or go on the rocks. I was "down," but I was not "out." I chanced to hear of a situation with an Indian Prince, who was in England for a holiday of seven months, with his suite, aidecamp, secretary, also a typewrighter or clerk, and two valets. I scarcely liked the idea at first, but eventually went to see him, and got the job as butler. He had a house in the West End of London. He told me to get some English servants, cook and housemaids, kitchenmaids. Money seemed to be plentiful, and no stint of anything in reason. They came to enjoy themselves, and they did. Polo, racehorses, theatres every night. Two cars were always outside the front door. It was a busy place. A dozen Indian officers would call at one time from Hampton Court. And I am not sure that some of the ladies that came to supper after the theatre were not pretty actresses. There were several old generals of the English army the Prince had met in India, and they were a thirsty lot. The Prince must have been a big bug in his own country. He did not speak to me at first, but always through his Aide de Camp, but after he got used to me, we often had a chat. He was of a splendid disposition, as sharp as a needle. His inteligence far surpassed any Englishman I ever met. When the troops marched past in front of Buckingham Palace after the War, the Prince stood by the side of the King on the dias, in his Indian uniform.

I was more of a house steward there, as I had to see to all supplies for the household. For the fancy dress balls at Covent Garden, and at the Albert Hall, he always had a box for his party, with two of us to wait on them. We enjoyed it quite as much as they did. It was very difficult to maintain any sort of order or regularity in the house, as the Indian servants had their meals at a different time than the other servants had theirs,

and the chauffeurs came in to meals at all times.
When motors were first used a lot of men learnt
to drive that knew nothing of the working of a
gentleman's house, and in most cases the old coachman either had to learn to drive, or get the sack.
These new class of men would come into the house,
smoke cigarettes, throws ends of cigarettes and
burnt matches all over the place.   Sometimes these
two chauffeurs had to wait an hour or two: by that
time the servants' hall would be like a tap room.
One of these chauffeurs was a curious character.
Suffice to say he was not an Englishman.   He
used to brag of the way he outwitted the officers in
bringing his revolver across from a country where
carrying arms was prohibited.   He was a terrible
swanker and bully.   He had never been in a gentleman's house before, and always carried his
loaded revolver.   I had great trouble in getting a
footman.   Of course all the young fellows had been
to the war, and were just returning.   If the poor
fellows knew anything of gentleman's service before they went, those that did not get killed seemed
to have forgotten what they did know.   I tried
several young fellows, but beyond smoking cigarettes, they knew very little.   Nothing of silver
cleaning, waiting, or the general duties of a house.
Eventually I got a tall young fellow, who looked
like a servant, but I soon found he would rather be
in the servants' hall smoking cigarettes with the

chauffeurs than work. I did manage to get him up in the dining room at meal times, but he did not know how to wait at table. He must have seen how the servants stood at a dinner party at the pictures, for all he did was to stand behind a chair and listen to the conversation. When the gentry laughed, he laughed, but he could not see a plate that wanted changing, or to hand the vegetables. In fact he was simply in the way. So as he would not take any interest, or take the trouble to learn, I had to get rid of him. My son had just been demobbed. In his early days he had been a footman, though now a chauffeur. I asked him if he would come up and give me a hand. He came, having not then got a job, though he hated indoor service. From that time I got on better. The chauffeur who carried the revolver made it a practice of coming to the front door, ringing the bell, when not with the car. I told him the area door was open and that he must go in that way. He began to bluster, said he would knock my b——y head off. I said I was not afraid of him, though he did carry a revolver. I watched his hand. If he had got his revolver out I should have smashed something in his face, a chair, vase, anything, and followed it up quickly. He did put his hand to his hip pocket, but he would never have fired that shot. (I did not know this till afterwards.) My son had been making up the fire in

the smoking room. On hearing the row he came
out to see what the trouble was, bringing a short
steel poker, with a round knob at the end. He
said that if the chauffeur had drawn his revolver
he would have broken his arm with it. The chauffeur did not know he was standing close behind
him. It is not often that affairs come to such
extremes as this: but it would not do to let such
people do as they like, or they would soon be "cock
of the walk."

The Indian Prince took a three months' lease of
a large Castle in Scotland for the grouse shooting, the property of a Noble Earl who wished to
let it, together with some of his servants.   So early
in August we went to Scotland. I had the greatest difficulty in keeping up supplies, as, not only
was whiskey and everything very scarce, but the
railway strike was on, but a merchant in the
nearest town came to my rescue. He managed
to get me almost everything I wanted, whether it
was in his line of business or not. There were
two brothers in the business, and very nice fellows
they were. The Prince managed to fill the Castle
with his friends, the old Generals, and a Raja and
his suite. There were plenty of servants, also
plenty to do. A chef and four maids in the kitchen, myself, and three waiters, two ushers, and an
odd man, besides the necessary housemaids. We
did not want any ladies-maids, as there were no

ladies.   There were seventeen gardeners.   On two
occasions the Prince sent his Aide de Camp to tell
me to keep a tighter hand over the drink.   I could
not understand this, as none of the servants were
ever the worse for it.   They had the usual allowance and no more, for I could not get an unlimited
supply.   When shooting on the moors the Prince
took his head Indian valet with him.   He had to
carry a leather case, containing square bottles,
each holding rather more than a bottle of whiskey
and port.   These bottles always came back to me
empty, to be filled again the next morning.   I
enquired of the Aide de Camp if the Prince generally used all the whiskey and port each day.
He said, "No, only perhaps one glass, sometimes
not at all."   Now "the cat was out of the bag."
It was the valet the Prince had noticed to be the
worse for drink.   After that he was not allowed
to take the case up to his room after returning
from shooting.   The Prince and Aide de Camp
were very abstemious, but the rest of the company
could put away any amount of champayne, whiskey, and port.   A car was kept solely to meet
every train to bring up everything.   They kept us
well supplied from Edinborough, though it took
a bit of manouvouring at that time.   The Prince
was always anxious to try all the Scotch dishes,
such as haggis, and other things.   Oysters were
served every night at dinner.   One day the Prince

told me to get fifty dozen oysters. They were to
have a competition to see who could eat the most.
I got them, and they set to work, with champayne.
The old Generals kept steadily on. I think one
of them won the wager, and scooped the pool.
The Paymaster (a Captain in the Indian Army)
made himself terribly ill. I got him to his bedroom, gave him some hot mustard and water, made
him sick, and put him to bed. None of them could
face oysters for dinner that night. The Prince
was very considerate to his servants. One day he
wished to give everyone who had served him in any
way a luncheon. They were all going to Edinborough by car that day. At such short notice I
could only muster fifty to sit down to luncheon.
We thoroughly enjoyed ourselves. There was
plenty of beer, whiskey, and pipes, tobacco, and
cigarettes. After lunch the tables were cleared
away. I got my violin to work. The Scotch are
passionately fond of dancing. We danced and
sang songs till six o'clock. The cost per head I
worked out at a little over ten shillings. The
Prince was very popular, and was liked by all who
knew him. People came with their autograph
books, asking if I could get him to sign his name,
which he did for several. As the time drew near
for us to return to London, we began to get our
things together for departure. The day was on
a Saturday. On the Thursday previous a 'phone

message came through from Balmorel, saying their
Majesties the King and Queen would come to the
Castle to lunch, on their way by car to London on
Friday. It was "all hands to the pump." A
sumptous luncheon was prepared, also for the
Equerries, and servants. The news got abroad
and people from miles around came and lined the
coachroad, which was more than a mile long.
They waited till five o'clock, when it was thought
that their Majesties had gone past without calling,
so it was a frost. Yet we had no further news
from Balmorel. On the Saturday morning the
Prince and the gentry departed to Edinborough.
I was to follow on as soon as I could with the servants. The motor lorry I had hired for our luggage had broken down in the coachroad. I was
enquiring where I could get another, as I wanted
to get to Edinborough before dark, when someone
shouted: "The King is coming." And shortly
after, sure enough, their cars drove up to the front
door. I had to explain matters. It appears there
had been a mistake as to date in the 'phone message. Luckily the fire had not gone out in the
dining room. We put more logs on. They had
luncheon baskets with them, so with that, and other
things (I sent up to the gardens for some grapes),
ending up with coffee. Their Majesties chatted
to me about the shooting, looked over the principal
rooms of the Castle, which was very historical, got

into their cars and away. The Queen shook hands
with me, and His Majesty left his photograph on
several pieces of paper for the servants. Had our
lorry not broken down we should all have been on
the road to Edinborough long before their Majesties got to the Castle. One can imagine the
Prince's disappointment on hearing the news,
when I arrived at the hotel where we were all to
stay that night, and on to London in the morning.
The rest of their visit to England was spent in
London. The Prince did the shopkeepers a good
turn, especially the jewellers. When, just before
they left for India, the Prince asked me to go with
him, I said I would have considered the proposition if I had been twenty years younger. He
said, "Why do you get old?" I replied, "Your
Highness, my life has not been such a bed of roses
that I should want to live it all over again." Independent of his Highness being very generous to
me, and all the English servants, he appreciated
all that I did for him, and what was more accept-
able, he treated me as though I was a human being.
It was a pleasure to serve him. I only wish they
were coming to England again. He could teach
English gentry a wrinkle or two as to the way
servants should be treated. Everyone was ever
anxious to do something for him. What a con-
trast to some of the English employers of servants.
When they begin calling them rude names, such

as, "You damned fool! You damned idiot!"
Why can't a servant reply in the same terms, or
something to this effect: "Thanks, same to you
with a piece of parsley on it." Oh, no, one must
not do that. If you only look as though you don't
like it, they will put in your "character" that you
are sulky and ill-tempered. Probably you would
never find out why, or what prevented a servant
from getting any given situation he applied for.
A servant's "character" is supposed to be a matter
of courtesy, a letter of confidence from the servant's last employer. They can say just what they
think fit, perhaps what is told them by an upper
servant, a confidential, treated as one of the family
sort of person, who has been watching, and probably has had her "knife in," to use a common
phrase, and has only been waiting her chance to
"rub one in" to the servant's injury. Or, take the
matter this way: A servant gives every satisfaction in her or his duties, but gives notice to leave;
circumstances may vary, but when her would be
employer applies for her "character" gets a reply
stating they do not wish to say anything about the
servant either way. They are so annoyed and vin-
dictive at her leaving them, they say to themselves,
if she or he will not work for us she shall not work
for anyone else. By doing this they do not lay
themselves open to any sort of claim, as gentry are
not bound in any way to give a servant a "charac-

ter," good, bad, or indifferent.   And you have no
remedy, as you remain ignorant as to why.   So
that you cannot bring an action for defamation of
character.

It reminds me of two children sitting on a door-
step.   One said, "Lend me your doll."   Margy
replied, "No, I want it myself."   Then the first
said, "If you won't lend me your doll I'll smash
it."

CHAPTER XIV

THERE was not much choice of places at this time, just after the Great War. Millions of men were out of work, so that after being at home for a week or two, I had to take a single-handed butler's place in the North of London, or continue to be out of work. So I said "Good-bye" to my blind wife, son, daughter-in-law, and boy, aged eight. I mention them all because of what befel them later. On arrival at the place I went into the pantry. On the wall facing me was a large card detailing my work for every hour of the day. I thought to myself, "What would the Trades Unions think of this little lot." I did not know whether to unpack my things, or bolt. This is a copy:—Commence work at 6.30 A. M. Open up the house. Sweep and dust the front hall. Clean dining room grate and light the fire. Clean boots, and do valeting by 7.30. Clean silver and lay breakfast by 8.15. Have own breakfast till 8.45. Clear dining room breakfast, wash up, and clean silver till 10.0. From 10.0 till 11.0 sweep dining room carpet, dust and polish the furniture and oak panneling. 11.0 till 12.0 clean silver and brass. Get dressed by 12.30. Serve lunch at 1.0. Every

Wednesday, 11.0 till 12, clean morning room silver and brass (forty ornamental pieces) besides other work above stated. Also wash out own glass and china cloths every day. Every Friday scrub floor tiles in front hall, clean brass candlabras and brass ornaments, and polish the furniture. Keep all fires up, and hearths swept tidy. Ring gong five minutes before each meal, and again five minutes later. Collect all dirty linen on Fridays, and exchange it for clean. Every Saturday turn out dining room thoroughly, polish oak pannelling and furniture every day. Every afternoon, finish cleaning all the silver. Answer all bells quickly. Be smart and clean in appearance. Every Sunday at 10.0 A.M. place tray on fancy cloth in dining room with whiskey, wine, cakes, and mineral waters, to remain there till lunch time. Keep all chairs on verandas dusted, see to sun blinds as required. All breakages to be mentioned at once. No visitors to servants, or smoking allowed. Not to remain in dining room after serving each course, as butler pulls the lift up and down for next course. Bring grog tray to smoking room at 9.30, with cakes. Take letters to post. Close all shutters, lock all doors, turn out all lights not required, do valeting, and go to bed by 10.30. Take all notes and messages when required. Butler's outings: Every Tuesday, after washing up lunch till 10.15 P.M. Every other Sunday, 2.30 till 10.15.

One day a month, after washing up breakfast and cleaning silver. (Leave everything clean and ready for maid to carry on.) The butler must be able to manage and keep all electric bells in order, also electric lights, trace defects, and put in new fuze wires. The butler must understand lavatory ball cocks, repair and glue furniture, also a knowledge of carpentering and painting. Wind all clocks once a week. Help take up, beat, and relay carpets. Keep own pantry clean, scrubbing floor and tables once a week. Answer the telephone quickly.

.   .   .   .

Now, there's a nice fifteen-hour day's work. The butler must never be out of hearing of the bells or telephone. If the telephone rang and was not answered it would not be long ere the butler heard of it. For perhaps the Mistress of the house would answer it afterwards, and one of her friends would say, "I rang up before, but could not make anyone hear." Then is the time to look out for "sparks." "Where were you that you did not answer the 'phone?" Curious to relate I remained in that place more than two years. One thing, there was no option, unless I wanted to be one of the unemployed, as butlers were not wanted: people could not afford to keep them. They are getting less and less, in fact will soon be as extinct as the Dodo. It would not be amis if the archiologists (or whatever they are called) were to get hold of a fine specimen, stuff him, and put him in the British Museum, put a label on him: "This was an English butler, fine specimen, warranted not to answer back." For I am sure he would be of more interest than these Egyptian mumies they are making a fuss about, whom we have never seen in life. Of course the place mentioned above was not the kind of service I had always been used to. There was the usual old and confidential servant. There is always one in every house who is encouraged to carry the news, it takes a little time to find them out, but when you have, "Beware." The cook was a curious specimen. She snuffled over her food. If there is anything I detest it is to sit down to meals with a person who snuffles over their food. Her uncle's niece was, or had been, an actress. This cook fancied actresses ran in the blood, for she thought she could sing (save the mark). On my right the old confidential would rave "Abide with me," as she professed to be religious. On my left the cook was raving out the "Soldier's March" from some old opera. By the time both had got well mixed it was difficult to tell what it was. But, taking this place on all points, they were very good to me, as long as I made myself adaptable to the conditions. Their bark was worse than their bite. The Bos told me I knew nothing about packing a suit case. He said shirts '(white starched ones) should be placed at the bottom of the box. I had always beeen taught to put the heavy things, such as boots, at the bottom, the lighter things on top. When we had finished and fastened up the case, I caught hold of the handle, and said, "Now, where are the shirts?" They were neither top nor bottom, but at the side of the case.

Even in the same house it may not be every department that gets "roasted." The housemaids may have a very good time of it; the kitchen people a rotten time; the pantry people have a very good time, and the ladies-maids get it hot, or visa-versa; or they may all get an outburst of temper from their employers all in their turn; just to let them know they are only servants, and very bad servants at that, and only a very inferior class of beings at the best.

About this time a dreadful calamity happened at home. My son's Bos made it a rule to send all his servants to the pantomime, by way of a treat. My son took his wife and boy with him. It was a cold and snowy night. On their coming out of the theatre they found it was still snowing. They were unable to get seats inside a 'bus, but eventually got seats outside. The next day they found they had all got influenza, or something worse. They were all in bed with it. My wife caught it, so that the whole household lay helpless in bed.

The doctor was sent for. He did not say exactly
what it was, but ordered in a day and night nurse,
also a woman to wait on them. My son's wife
went unconscious, and remained so. My wife died
of it. My son pulled through after a fortnight,
also his son got better, but a few days after caught
the measles; yet he had never been out of the house.
He had to be isolated. My son's wife went near
to death's door; in fact, on two occasions, I thought
she was really dead. She went to a mere skeleton,
just skin and bone. The crisis came. The doctor
said if she lived that night there would be hopes.
What with the cylinders of hydrogen, the nurses,
my wife's funeral, and one thing and another, I
thought to myself, "Was there ever such a house?"
Luckily, I had drawn a hundred pounds, my insurance in the Prudential, or I don't know where
we should have been. All this through going to
see a pantomime. My son's wife turned the danger point, and from that time, though still unconscious, began to mend. It took months before she
got on her feet again, and the nurses out of the
house. The doctor said it was the most miraculous
cure he ever knew. The boy got over the measles
and got strong again, but he terribly misses his old
granny.

It is remarkable how some servants put on
"side," and swank after they have got on a bit, and
got a show of decent clothes together. One such

case occurred in a place that I lived in. This
swanky housemaid gave out that her father was a
farm baliff in Blankshire. Happening to be visiting at a place near I thought I would walk over
to the farm, and see her father.

Seeing some men standing in the farmyard, I
enquired if Mr. Soandso, calling him by name, the
farm baliff was about. "There is no farm baliff
by that name; you mean old Joe, the carter."
Some servants suffer badly from swelled head, and
are ashamed of their humble origin. At another
farm the supply of eggs had reduced considerably.
The estate agent called on the farm hand who had
charge of the chicken, at his cottage to explain
the shortage. The farm hand happened to be at
his breakfast. The agent called him out, and
asked if he could give any reason. "I dunno why
it is, sir," said Giles. "I hope you don't think I
have been taking them, sir, for it's months since
I have even tasted an egg." "Then it is a devil of
a long time since you washed your face," replied
the agent, "for your mouth is covered with egg
now." Moral: Always use a serviette.

.   .   .   .

Thinking, after two years, that I could be doing
better than in a single-handed place, I gave in a
month's notice to leave. There, in that, I soon
found I had made a mistake. I soon found there

was a glut of unemployed butlers, and no places
to be had, and as "Half a loaf is better than no
bread," I found I had better have staid where I
was. I advertised every week in the *Morning
Post,* searched all the clubs in the West End of
London, and all places where butler's places are
likely to be heard of, but to no effect. Excepting
for a month's temporary work, I have had no employment for months. Everywhere it is parlourmaids, and married couples that are wanted. The
married couples having to do the work of perhaps
four servants that were kept previously. If they
have given up their house or rooms, and don't like
the place, they are bound to stop, for there are no
rooms or houses to be had. So that their employers have got them fairly by the neck. The married couple can't turn out and sleep by the road-
side, especially so in winter time.

Before the Great War gentry did not think it
the fashion to wear old and shabby clothes. Now
they make them last as long as they possibly can.
A man called at a certain tailor's shop in the West
End, mentioning a gentleman's name. The
tailor's man, thinking he was the valet, said, "We
have not had Mr Whatsisname's on our books
lately. Does he get his clothes anywhere else?"
"No," replied the man, "I don't think so."
"Well, here's half a sovereign, and a wire brush;

slip that into his clothes briskly, and we shall soon have him here for some new ones!" The man was Mr Whatsisname himself.

.   .   .   .

I have been thinking a ladies daily life might be called playing at a game of "Flop." Firstly, she flops out of bed, and flops into a bath, flops into a chair fronting a mirror, flops into a chair at the breakfast table, after breakfast flops into a chair and bullies the servants, flops into her car, flops into a chair at her dressmakers, or a shop counter, again flops into her car, flops into a chair for lunch, then flops into a chair or sofa in the drawing room, flops into her car, flops into an easy chair in someone's drawing room, again flops into her car, goes to matinee, flops into a stall, afterwards flops into her car, goes home, flops into a chair for tea, flops into a chair fronting a mirror, flops into a chair for dinner, flops on a sofa in the drawing room, when she gets tired of that flops into a bath, and flops into bed.

A great many of the gentry take very little interest in their children; in fact, in some cases they are looked upon as an infernal nusiance. They are brought to the drawing room for the mother to see if the nurse keeps them clean and tidy once a day. And when they are old enough, are bundled off to some school, to Harrow and Eton if they are rich enough. The mother, with all her flopping to do, has no time to bother about her children. If they think so little of their children how much less do they think of their servants? I will give an instance. In the early part of this year, I interviewed a certain titled lady, living not a dozen miles from Buckingham Palace.

It was for a six weeks' job, as the family were going to the sea-side. Everything being satisfactory, she engaged me, and told me she would let me know what day to come and take the plate and things down, and get ready for them at the sea-side house. I waited till the day they were to leave London, but got no word from her. So early in the morning I called at the house. The servant said that her Ladyship had gone to the seaside the day previous, taking a butler—I suppose, a cheaper man—with her. His Lordship, who was at home, refused to see me, but sent to say he left all household affairs to her Ladyship. I obtained their sea-side address, wrote her a letter, asking for at least a week's pay, as she had prevented me from applying for another situation. I waited a week, but got no reply. I then again wrote, pointing out that my claim would be upheld in a Court of Law. Still I got no reply. She knew I had no written agreement, and at the interview I foolishly handed her letter to me back to her, which she kept. It would simply mean my word against hers, and the weakest always goes to the wall. Even if I had brought an action my name would have become known in the case, and I should never have got another place. The gentry are so clanish. Still, she has my wish, which is: "May they perish," for treating a working man in such a fashion. The inconvenience she had caused me, the cost of my railway fares, were of no more consideration to her than a piece of dirt sticking to the heel of her boot. It is this sort of treatment to servants that makes them take such a dislike to the game. If the employers only knew the value of a kind word, they would be more liberal with them. They would get a great deal more work done, and willing work too.

CHAPTER XV

A CERTAIN Duke stood on a hill looking at his vast estate: as far as he could see was his property. He observed to his agent: "Lovely scenery, is it not? Yet I cannot eat or drink it, or take it with me when I die. You, or anyone else, may look at it, and that is all I can do." But what would the estate look like if he had not agent, farm steward, and labourers to look after it, and gamekeepers to protect his game, servants to obey his every wish. The whole place would simply be a curse to him. Later on he came across a stranger on his land, and asked him if he knew he was trespassing on his land. "Your land," said the stranger; "how do you make it out to be your land?" The Duke said, "I inherited it from my father, and have every right to it." "And, pray, where did your father get it?" "He got it from his ancestors, who fought for it." "Then," said the stranger, "it's about time it was fought for again. Come on!"

These great landowners are very jealous of their estates; they would not lose an inch of it. But they are not so particular as to the way they add

to it when they can see a chance. I will point out
an instance. When I was a boy my uncle held a
small farm not many miles from Southampton,
on the borders of a rich man's estate—a small
stream devided it from the park. My aunt was
my father's sister: they had a few cows, pigs, a
lot of chicken, an old horse or two. My uncle was
churchwarden or something of the sort. Nothing
pleased me better than to walk the five miles to
visit them on a Sunday when the fruit was ripe in
the orchard; they would lend me an old muzzle-
loading gun, powder, shot and caps, and I would
shoot the thrushes and blackbirds that came to eat
the cherries. I generally ate too much fruit, and
got stomach ache. It was a fine old thatched
house. Its surroundings would be a fine subject
for a painter of pictures. The scene was painted
by Ward, in 1831. I have the oil painting, a sun-
light effect, in my posesion. My uncle and aunt
made enough to live comfortably, in spite of the
ravages of rabbits from the rich man's estate adjoining, also of the phesants. They must have oc-
cupied the farm for twenty-five years when my
uncle died. My aunt carried on for some few
years, hiring extra help, employing an extra farm
hand. But now came the rich man's chance. He
turned her out of the farm, as he wanted the land
added to his park, pulled down the old farmhouse.
My aunt went to a cottage in the village, and died

in less than three months. My aunt was the only
person I ever heard use the old expression,
"Marry come up." The kitchen was lighted by
diamond paned windows, the floor was red bricks,
the great wide fireplace with seats each side the
fire which was on the hearth, no grate, fire-dogs
each side, a chain and hook, a three-legged pot,
sides of bacon hung up the chimney. Potatoes
and cabbage, in nets, were cooked with bacon in
the three-legged pot.

I observed in the newspaper a year or so after
the great war a certain lady of prominence wrote
an article saying the poor were behaving as though
they were the cream of the land, whereas they
were only the scum. It was during the time of the
great labour strikes. I should like to ask her
which is the scum: the busy bee who gathers the
honey, or the drone who brings no honey to the
hive? For she certainly belongs to the latter class,
who lives on what the workers produce, directly
or indirectly. Did she ever produce anything but
talk, and such talk as that simply widens the gulf
between the worker and those that do not work, the
rich and the poor. Was her money amassed without the aid of the worker? and does she not live
on what the worker produced? These things may
not have been accomplished in her generation, but
it must have been done some time previously, for
in all labour there is profit, so without labour there

is no profit. Did she ever do a hard day's work
in her life? Useful work. Fancy seeing her on
her knees, with a slavey's cap and coarse apron on,
blackleading a grate, but worse still, having to
live in the same house with a person of her
ideas of human nature. Scum indeed! What is
wanted in this country is a leader whose body and
soul is for the good of the workers (the parasites
can look after themselves); the busy bees, the
honey makers, are the ones to take first consideration, and everything else would follow that the
country desires, health, wealth, happiness, content-
ment. Whereas now it is nothing but discontent-
ment all round.

But where are we to find the strong man with
gumption and originality? Not at Westminster:
I am afraid not. I have lived amongst the class
that Members of Parliament are drawn from, all
my life: have seen their inner life. As for intelect:
God help them. All they learnt at school and
college was to act like a gentleman, but that does
not prove that they are gentlemen. Certainly
they do not view the problem of life from the same
standpoint as the worker views it. Then how can
they be expected to mix a plaster to suit the workers' case?

A man in his own district in the country may be
of small importance, but when he puts up for
Parliment and gets M.P. tacked on to his name

he immediately becomes a big bug, and the way they go about it is at least peculiar, to say the least of it.

I will give an instance. I was living in the service of the gentleman who was "entering the lists," for a constituency in the North of England. It was several years before the war, at the time there was a great outcry about so many foreigners being employed in this country, and so many Britishers walking about without a job. At the election speeches this question was brought forward. My Bos said he would give the matter his special attention should they give him their votes and put him in Parliment, which eventually they did. Now at that very moment he employed in his house a German housekeeper, a French chef, a German under housemaid, and a Swiss under housemaid, and a French ladies-maid. There is no length they will not go with safety to get the M. P. tacked on to their names.

I was staying in another large house where another seat in Parliment was to be contested. The would be member's wife was helping him by visiting all the people's houses who had a vote. The party were ready to start, the carriage being at the door, when the lady sent for her maid upstairs for some extra pairs of white gloves, then, turning to the other visitors, observed: "To shake hands with common herd." If there happened to be a baby in the voter's houses the lady would exclaim, "Oh, what a lovely child," and would kiss the child all over if only votes were promiced her husband at the election. And the husband on his part has all of a sudden become extremely affable. On meeting a voter he shook hands and said, "Well, Jiles, how are things going with you?" Yet, whether that gentleman got into Parliment or did not, one thing is very certain: when he meets Jiles, or any of the voters who put him where he is, they have grown so darned small that neither he or his wife can see them. If I were asked what I am, a Conservative, a Liberal, a Wee Free, or all the rest of it, I could not tell them. I am just what a life lived amongst the Aristocracy has made me. I certainly do not believe in Socialism in its crude state.

It lies in the power of upper servants either to make the younger ones lives livable, or a perfect hell. When one considers that in a large house there are servants whose dispositions are all different. They have got to live peacably with one another. There may be Swiss, French, Italian, Belgians, Irish, Scotch, Welsh, English, and before the war, Germans galore. It resembles a lot of squirrels in a cage with a wheel. The employer says, "There you are, then; spin away, you devils." It is simply a matter of temperament in the individual, whether he or she can adapt themselves to the conditions or not. In some situations the servants are very happy, in others just the reverse. There is this difference: In any trade or other profession, one has to be with objectionable people only during working hours. In service one has to be with them, living always in the same house, night and day, Sundays and weekdays.

It is an old saying that Like likes Like. No honest, truthful, straightforward man or woman likes a lying, two-faced person. Neither does a lying, deceitful person like a straightforward, trustworthy, truthful man or woman. But they think them fair game to be shot at. The lying deceiver gets on well in gentleman's service, for a time, perhaps a long time, untill they are found out. They can always spin a plausible tale, pleasing to their employers, to whom the truth is often distasteful. But consider the damage they have done to others in the house before they *are* found out.

Jealousy, backbiting, slandering is only natural where a lot of servants are shut up in a house together, with the same hum-drum duties to do day after day. There is not enough variety of thought to distract their attention from it, during the long day, without amusements or freedom. The shop girl, or factory girl may have to work hard, but she does not have to begin work at five-thirty and keep on more or less continually till ten-thirty at night, as I know of some housemaids who do it in the winter. The outdoor girl can look forward to the time she will finish for the day, probably at five or six in the evening.

The employer does not trouble himself what they do or where they go; as soon as they are outside the place they are free. All that is required is that they shall be back to time on the following morning.

The National Insurance scheme is a farce as far as servants are concerned. If a servant does not feel well, can he or she leave their work and join up in the queue to see the doctor at 9 A. M. or at 6 P. M., the surgery hours? Most likely be away an hour. They may do it once, but will soon get the order of the "Boot," as the gentry will not have unhealthy servants in their houses. Most of them are most unnatural on this point. For instance, a noble Lord I served, whose butler fell ill with pains in the stomach. The butler saw a doctor but got no better and could not do his work. The Noble Lord said, "Is not that fellow any better?" As he did not appear to wait at table after the second day the Noble Lord called in his own doctor, who ordered him to be taken (after consulation with the Noble Lord) to St. George's Hospital, on a Sunday afternoon.

The butler died there in less than a week. The same Noble Lord treated his valet, who had been with him over twenty years, in a similar way.   The valet fell ill.   The Noble Lord had his own doctor to examine him.   Said it was heart disease. The valet was at once turned out of the house. He took a quiet, single-handed butler's place. He died in less than a month.   The Noble Lord would not allow a servant to die in his house. Now, if this had been one of his hunters that was sick, there would have been no end of a fuss.

I call to mind an event that occurred at a small place in the North of London, where a butler and five maids were kept.   The cook took the place as her sweetheart was a chaffeur living within walking distance, and naturally wanted to see each other sometimes, as sweethearts have done since the world began.   Having finished her work after supper, she popped up to the side gate for a few minutes' chat, and to rub noses, as he was not allowed in the house.   Some of the girls gave her away to the "Missus," who sent all the other maids to bed, and told the butler to stand by, in case of a disturbance.   The cook appeared, well before the time the house was usually locked up, and was met by the "Missus" at the side door.   They bundled her out of the house that night, and sent her boxes after her next day.   She was a capable cook, and a well educated girl, but what humiliation.   In another place, on the opposite side of London, cook after cook left because "No visitors allowed" was the order.   So the employers gave in at last: they had to allow the girls' sweethearts in or cook their own food.   Consequently when the Lady went into the kitchen there sat the man in the arm chair, and did not even stand up and make his observance of respect, but told them if he was not to be allowed in he should take the cook away.   This sort of thing frequently occurs in small places.

I have not written much about maidservants, for they can generally speak for themselves.   As regard cooks, I have met those who has been plesant to work with, also the reverse.   Some of them ought to have a piece of red ribbon tied on behind, similar to that on a horse in the hunting field, or racing paddock.   For one never knows when they are going to "lash out."   As regards ladies-maids, they would be disappointed if, when they have "got 'em all on," with a touch of the powder puff, they were not taken for real ladies. They abhor having to go in and out of the area gate, but would much rather use the front door. In fact it would be difficult to tell now-a-days which was the ladies-maid and which was the Lady of the house, when out walking.   Even the scullery maid must dress herself in the height of fashion, when it is her Sunday out.   Forty years ago servants were not allowed to wear a hat, but only a demure bonnet.

It would be difficult to tell that a char lady was a char lady, for she too must dress in the fashion when out of doors, as far as her pocket will permit. I have seldom met one that has not seen better days. Life must be hard for them to have to do it. Probably she has to pay a neighbour a shilling a day to see that her children get their dinner when they come home from school. Her husband perhaps out of work. Did anyone see a crosseyed servant? No, they are as scarce as dead donkeys. A servant must be absolutely perfect in form, disposition, and action. He must have no sweaty, smelly skin, or feet, which a great many people have. There used to be an old titled lady in Eaton Place who was very prowd of her two tall match footmen. When she was engaging them she would make them walk backwards and forwards across the room to see if she liked their action, just as though she was buying a horse; the footman also had to open the door, go out, and come into the room again, to show if he did it properly. No, a servant must not be knock-kneed, flat-footed, humpty-backed, or idiotic, neither do they like the bald headed ones, they must be properly thatched. In some places they will have all their men with hair of the same colour, either all light or all dark.

Of course a tall man has the preference, and advantage of a shorter man in service. Had I been three inches taller, a six-foot man, I could easily have got to the very top of the tree. The experience was there. The first-class character was there, but in a first-class place a six-foot man would be taken in preference to me. Though I have never had to borrow a penny in my life, I cannot say I am much better off than when I began in gentleman's service.

When my brother kept the shop in the Fulham Road an old butler, who was in the workhouse, used to leave an old private coat and hat with my brother to take care of. When it was his day out he came there and changed his workhouse clothes, and no wonder, after being in gentleman's service, among the Aristocracy all his life. People remark, why did he not take care and save his money when he was in service? But I say, if a man has a family and wife to keep, and house rent to pay, there is not much left out of a wage of seventy or eighty pounds a year, finding his own clothes. If a servant is an honest man and has to do the above, he will be worse off at the end of thirty years' service than when he began. He may, if he is a single man all his life, manage to keep out of the work house at the end, but he would have to be lucky, and have found good situations. Perhaps one in a hundred butlers gets a sort of pension, enough to keep him out of the workhouse.

I have had chances of taking valuable things in

my time, that would never have been missed, because no one knew they were there, but a clear
conscience is of much more value, and if I must
die in the workhouse, I must.   After having had
fifty years of it, I still keep the old flag flying, and
feel as fit as most men at thirty, and say:

"It's easy enough to be pleasant
When life goes by like a song,
But the man worth while, is the man with a smile
When everything goes dead wrong."

Au Revoir